# Who's Minding the Store?

# The Report *of The*
# Twentieth Century Fund
# Task Force *on*
# Market Speculation *and*
# Corporate Governance

With Background Paper
## Who's Minding the Store?
## by Robert J. Shiller

The Twentieth Century Fund Press/New York/1992

The Twentieth Century Fund is a research foundation undertaking timely analyses of economic, political, and social issues. Not-for-profit and nonpartisan, the Fund was founded in 1919 and endowed by Edward A. Filene.

BOARD OF TRUSTEES OF THE TWENTIETH CENTURY FUND

Morris B. Abram, *Emeritus*

H. Brandt Ayers

Peter A. A. Berle

José A. Cabranes

Joseph A. Califano, Jr.

Alexander Morgan Capron

Hodding Carter III

Edward E. David, Jr.

Brewster C. Denny, *Chairman*

Charles V. Hamilton

August Heckscher, *Emeritus*

Matina S. Horner

Lewis B. Kaden

Madeleine May Kunin

James A. Leach

Richard C. Leone, *ex officio*

P. Michael Pitfield

Don K. Price, *Emeritus*

Richard Ravitch

Arthur M. Schlesinger, Jr., *Emeritus*

Harvey I. Sloane, M.D.

Theodore C. Sorensen

James Tobin, *Emeritus*

David B. Truman, *Emeritus*

Shirley Williams

William Julius Wilson

Richard C. Leone, *President*

Library of Congress Cataloging-in-Publication Data

The Report of the Twentieth Century Fund Task Force on Market Speculation and Corporate Governance.
    p.    cm.
    "With background paper, Who's minding the store? by Robert J. Shiller."
    Includes bibliographical references and index.
    ISBN 0-87078-330-0
    1. Corporations—United States—Finance. 2. Corporations—United States—Growth. 3. Corporate governance—United States. 4. Speculation—United States. 5. Institutional investments—United States. I. Shiller, Robert J. Who's Minding the store? 1992. II. Twentieth Century Fund. Task Force on Market Speculation and Corporate Governance.
HG4061.R46      1992
338.7'4'0973—dc20                                                     92-34936
                                                                         CIP

Cover Design and Illustration: Claude Goodwin
Manufactured in the United States of America.
Copyright © 1992 by the Twentieth Century Fund, Inc.

# Foreword

The great theme of the national political campaign of 1992, obvious through the steady stream of gossip and mudslinging, was how to get the American economy moving again. When they weren't talking about the economy, the candidates stressed the importance of trust. In this latter emphasis, they may have been more on target than they knew. For it is probably true that "trust," in the broadest sense, is one of the necessary prerequisites for restructuring the U.S. economy. Without increased trust in their leaders, the voting public and corporate shareholders alike—lacking the confidence to forgo current rewards while awaiting the larger slice of the pie that might come later from wise investment—will continue to think only in terms of short-term gain and loss.

During the decade of the 1980s, the glamour and scope of financial markets and financial "deals" masked the fact that they seldom addressed the issues of real economic growth. In fact, since 1973, productivity growth in the United States has been relatively sluggish. In the past dozen years, four-fifths of American workers suffered declines in real wages, more single-earner families became impoverished, and income distribution became more unequal. Our children perform poorly on tests of science and math, our products face increasing international competition, and our savings rate is near the bottom among industrialized countries. Our infrastructure is deteriorating faster than it is being maintained or replaced. The long-term solutions to all these problems, of course, are rooted in training, innovation, and investment; the last, as noted, may well be dependent on the restoration of a degree of trust.

But it is also true that, in a more narrow sense, our jobs, wages, and interest and dividend income often depend on the success or failure of large corporations. Corporate performance in turn depends on the decisions made by managers. And, as Adolf A. Berle, Jr., and Gardiner Means pointed out more than a half-century ago, managers' interests and shareholders' interests may not coincide; they may even be in conflict. Managers pursue their goals under the supervision of directors and within the constraints of market forces. In theory, a manager who does not get the highest feasible returns from a firm's assets will be sacked by the directors, or the firm will be acquired through financial markets by those who realize the full potential for the owners. As we know too well, the accountability described in this kind of model ignores some of the real world imperfections of the marketplace, as well as aspects of the behavior of the human beings involved. In a world of institutional investors, junk bonds, and leveraged buyouts—a world in which managers, bankers, lawyers, and even directors can be co-opted by the staggering payouts that come from ownership changes—there are plenty of reasons to ask whether the system is working as well as it should.

It often seems that our best and brightest are being drawn to the paper economy, not to activities that would resolve these central problems more directly. At best, financial services can lubricate the wheels of investment and innovation, not replace them. When the goal of traders and portfolio managers is short-term capital gains, what happens to the executive whose sights are set on more distant targets? Will financial markets give an innovator or a good production manager enough time to build up the flow of profits? Amidst all this excitement about quarterly performance, is anyone looking to the long run?

Managers may receive perverse incentives from the market. The principal pressure on a corporate executive is to increase the value of stockholders' equity. In financial markets dominated by institutional investors, this incentive can malfunction. Presently, institutional portfolio managers closely track short-term movements of stock prices, trying to choose the best moments for their frequent transactions. A principal criterion for judging a firm's performance may be rumors about its attractiveness to takeover specialists. With few exceptions, these financiers are disengaged from corporate decisionmaking, even if they control substantial blocks of stock; they "vote" with their purchases and sales of financial assets. Election of corporate directors and selection of executives rarely attract the active involvement of pension and mutual funds. Constant concern with short-term performance and stock prices, imposed by market forces, can foreshorten an executive's horizons, undermining his or her ability to deal with fundamental problems.

In fact, a considerable literature now exists exploring the notion that American markets, corporate culture, and even general life style have contributed to a phenomenon called short-termism, an emphasis on immediate return rather than investment and growth. At the same time, the vast increase in the size and variety of instruments in the equity, debt, and other financial markets has been accompanied by a concern about whether the volatility of such markets has a negative impact on the real economy.

In this context, the Twentieth Century Fund decided to convene a diverse group of business leaders, academics, and analysts to look at a series of questions about our financial markets and corporate governance. The basic question was whether the current system was contributing as much as possible to the solution of our real economic problems, such as producing jobs, increasing productivity, and sharpening competitiveness. The group also asked a series of questions about the potential for change in the marketplace and the board room: How can we modify financial markets to produce incentives for better corporate management? Can the goal of improved governance be accomplished while at the same time cutting the significant costs associated with financial transactions, including market overhead, legal, and transaction fees? Would greater investment by institutional investors in corporate decisionmaking—so-called relationship investing—be beneficial? The Task Force spent considerable time discussing this last question, and indeed generally supported the concept. The group recognized, however, that a full analysis of its pros and cons was beyond its scope.

Robert J. Shiller, Stanley B. Resor Professor of Economics at Yale University, wrote the background paper for the group and served as Task Force executive director. The sessions were admirably led by the group's chair, Lewis B. Kaden, a partner at Davis Polk & Wardell. Bernard Wasow, a counsultant to the Fund and associate professor of economics at New York University, served as Fund liaison with the members of the Task Force and contributed significantly to its work. Their contributions and those of all the members can best be measured by the extraordinary complexity of the issues they confronted. The Fund is very much in their debt.

One thing is certain: the American economy is astonishing in its diversity. It defies generalization. Even the most rigorous analysis of this marketplace may produce ambiguous results. None of these characteristics inhibit a constant and lively debate about where we are and where we are headed economically. The questions we face are so difficult that it is probably impossible to find definitive answers to them. The economist's model necessarily excludes key elements. Studies of economic history incorporate many of the factors that contribute to outcomes, but raise other difficulties in terms of idiosyncrasy or generalization. In the end, we must find a way to think and act in these areas based on the best judgment available. The pages that follow, we think, provide an excellent example of what that sort of inquiry can produce.

Richard C. Leone, *President*
The Twentieth Century Fund
November 1992

# Contents

| | |
|---|---|
| **Foreword** by Richard C. Leone | v |
| **Task Force Members** | xi |
| **Report of the Task Force** | 1 |
| **Dissent** by James Tobin | 23 |
| **Comment** by Horace J. DePodwin | 24 |
| **Who's Minding the Store?**<br>Background Paper by Robert J. Shiller | 27 |
| Introduction | 29 |
| Chapter One: Speculation and Market Volatility | 33 |
| Chapter Two: Recent Concerns and Policy Proposals | 39 |
| Chapter Three: Speculation and Economic Theory | 45 |
| Chapter Four: Today's Concerns with Speculative Behavior | 61 |
| Chapter Five: Measures for Dealing with Speculation and Short-Termism | 85 |
| Chapter Six: Discount Rates and Saving Rates | 95 |
| Chapter Seven: Conclusion: Sorting Through an Array of Policy Options | 105 |
| Notes | 111 |
| Bibliography | 125 |
| Index | 137 |
| About the Author | 143 |

# Task Force Members

**Lewis B. Kaden,** *Task Force Chair*
Partner
Davis Polk & Wardwell

**Horace J. DePodwin**
President
Economic Studies, Inc.

**Joseph S. DiMartino**
President and Chief Operating
    Officer
The Dreyfus Corporation

**C. Austin Fitts**
President
The Hamilton Securities Group, Inc.

**Benjamin M. Friedman**
William Joseph Maier Professor of
    Political Economy and Chairman
Department of Economics
Harvard University

**Stephen J. Friedman**
Executive Vice President and
    General Counsel
The Equitable Life Assurance Society
    of the United States of America

**James Grant**
Editor
*Grant's Interest Rate Observer*

**Louis Lowenstein**
Simon H. Rifkind Professor of
    Finance and Law
Columbia University Law School

**Roland M. Machold**
Director
New Jersey Division of Investment

**Robin Illgen Neustein**
Partner
Goldman, Sachs & Co.

**Martin J. Rabinowitz**
General Partner
Odyssey Partners, L.P.

**Muriel F. Siebert**
President
Muriel Siebert & Co., Inc.

**Leonard Silk**
Former Economics Columnist
*The New York Times*
Adjunct Professor
Graduate School and University
    Center
City University of New York

**Richard F. Syron**
President and Chief Executive Officer
Federal Reserve Bank of Boston

**James Tobin**
Sterling Professor Emeritus of
  Economics
Cowles Foundation for Research in
  Economics
Yale University

**Barrie A. Wigmore**
Limited Partner
The Goldman Sachs Group, L.P.

**Robert J. Shiller,** *Task Force*
*Executive Director*
Stanley B. Resor Professor of
  Economics
Cowles Foundation for Research in
  Economics
Yale University

# Report of the Task Force

The United States economy and financial system suffer from "short-termism," an affliction caused by a lack of attention to long-term economic performance. Financial markets put pressure on corporate managers to focus too much on quarterly profits and too little on patient investment for the long haul.

Responsibility for a corporation's future is in the hands of three groups: corporate managers, board directors, and investors. But often, none of these groups ranks the long term as its highest priority. Corporate executives, who do not themselves own their companies, are often judged by others on how well they meet short-term objectives. Boards of directors, who have the responsibility for overseeing management performance and setting long-term organizational strategic directions, often have neither the time nor the inclination to supervise seriously management decisionmaking. And the primarily institutional investors who really do own the corporation are rewarded in part on the basis of the profit they reap from short-term price changes, which can make them more likely to focus on short-term trading decisions than on the organization's long-term problems and prospects. The result—in too many instances—is that neither managers, directors, nor owners are minding the store.

The problem of short-termism is neither new nor the sort of national crisis that excites the popular imagination. After all, its effects will not be felt until some time in the future. Short-termism in finance and corporate planning, however, deserves attention because it is part of a larger pattern in which finance flourishes while our real economic foundation slowly erodes. In the 1980s, America's financial markets soared, fed by a surge of corporate takeovers and restructuring. For a while, it seemed as if financial deals alone could create real purchasing power. But even during those heady years, the real income of ordinary people stagnated. Perhaps the spotlight on financial superstars blinded the nation to such long-term, structural problems in the real economy as slow productivity growth, falling saving rates, inadequate educational and health-care systems, growing extremes of wealth and poverty, and the enormous burden of public and private debt. Today, these real economic problems threaten our standing in a world of intensifying global economic competition.

The members of this Task Force therefore recommend that the connection between long-term performance and economic rewards be tightened. The time has passed for Americans to accept speculative excesses in finance coupled with underinvestment in productive capacity and management that receives personal rewards barely connected to real economic results.* Unfortunately, traditional methods of oversight—including existing mechanisms for shareholder voice, outside director supervision of management, and derivative litigation—although useful, seem to have proved inadequate to the task. The question thus is, What changes in our laws, regulatory structures, and corporate culture will help channel the skill and energy of our financial and managerial elite toward long-run performance rather than short-term appearances?

Many in academic, corporate, and financial circles are involved in intense debate over the operation of financial markets, the current system of corporate governance, and the links between market practice and corporate performance. The relative merits of legislative and regulatory reform are also hotly contested. The participants in these debates generally start from certain common ground: liquid financial markets are good for the economy; a long-term perspective by investors and managers enhances corporate performance; and international competition increasingly will compel us to examine the relationship between financial markets and corporate governance.

Once past these simple precepts, the debate quickly becomes contentious. Many academic observers deny that there is a problem of short-termism. They offer some valid arguments about the ability of our financial system to deal with long-term problems. Even if stock market investors are in the market only for the short term, the argument goes, they have ample reason for taking long-term problems into account when deciding where to invest: those problems may become apparent before they sell their stock, thereby reducing the market price. So, anticipating future difficulties, investors may decide to sell today. As a result, a company neglectful of the long term may see its share price decline immediately. The corporation may thus be unable to raise any more resources in financial markets for further investments. It may be taken over by

---

* *Martin J. Rabinowitz* does not believe that American industry generally has underinvested in productive capacity.

another firm. To the extent that share prices immediately and accurately reflect long-term prospects and problems, top managers who are rewarded with bonuses and stock options tied to share price have an incentive to be concerned about the long term.

**In spite of how attractive these theoretical arguments sound, the Task Force believes that our financial markets do not encourage executives and investors to take full account of the long term.** We believe that decision horizons are often too short, that corporate managers expend too much effort on cosmetic adjustments to quarterly earnings reports, and that since financial markets boom and crash, often for no sensible reason, short-term ups and downs are erratic guides for corporate policies. **The Task Force therefore believes that reforming incentives for taking a long-term perspective will make a great difference in our economic success in coming decades.**

Doing so, however, presents a problem, because opinions vary sharply about the effectiveness of different reforms and about the ability of public policy to contribute to efficient markets, effective corporate governance, and competitive products and services. Clearly, some problems cannot be addressed by changes in law or regulatory policy. For example, fundamental habits in the corporate culture cannot be eliminated through a few government interventions. But there are measures that we can take as a nation to encourage behavior that enhances economic performance. And although we should not copy those whose cultures are very different from ours, we can learn from the institutions and practices of our trading partners and competitors so long as we understand that what we learn must be adapted to our own traditions to be effective.

This Task Force—composed of active participants and experts on financial markets and the corporate sector—brought varied points of view and experience to the evaluation of these problems and discussed a wide array of policies for financial markets and corporate governance. The Task Force has reached both positive and negative conclusions, sometimes agreeing with and other times disputing the conventional wisdom. The Task Force, judging some of the most fashionable proposals for policy reform to be of doubtful value, has drawn its own conclusions. Put briefly, **the Task Force's principal recommendations are**:

- ◆ **Remedies for "short-termism" should be sought principally in reforms of corporate governance.**

  - ▲ **Owners of public corporations should provide more active oversight and should participate more in management.**

6 ◆ WHO'S MINDING THE STORE?

  - ▲ **This goal should be pursued mainly through encouragement of "relational investing." Large shareholders and fiduciaries (especially pension funds) should become more involved in monitoring corporate management.**

  - ▲ **Regulations and tax and accounting rules all should be revised to permit and encourage relational investing.**

  - ▲ **Additional disclosure of executive pay and benefits along the lines recently approved by the SEC should prove beneficial.**

  - ▲ **Relaxing rules that restrict shareholder communication, also along the lines approved by the SEC, should also prove helpful.**

  - ▲ **"Corporate Democracy" and "Shareholder Rights," while clearly useful, are not a sufficiently effective approach to the problem.**

- ◆ **Some commonly suggested direct measures to discourage high turnover and hinder the formation of speculative bubbles in financial markets—transaction taxes, additional circuit breakers—hold little promise for encouraging long-term investing.**

- ◆ **Tax reform is needed, both to achieve the goals summarized above and to encourage productive investment.**[*]

  - ▲ **The tax on capital gains should be graduated steeply according to holding period. The rate on short-term holdings should be raised and the rate on long-term holdings lowered.**

---

[*] In addition to these recommendations, many members of the Task Force agreed that public sector dissaving to finance current spending must be reduced in order to reduce real interest rates and thereby the cost of capital; in other words, our persistent structural public budget deficits must be controlled.

▲ **Debt and equity should be treated equally in corporate taxation. To this end, the deductibility of corporate interest costs should be effectively eliminated and the tax rate on corporate profits should be reduced correspondingly to maintain revenue neutrality.**

## An In-Depth Exploration of the Recommendations

High-volume, speculative trading and short-lived bubbles and crashes are seen by many as the essence of "short-termism." Most policy discussions of the problem begin with measures to tax transactions, to limit the introduction of new products, or otherwise to "throw sand in the wheels" of financial markets. We see high turnover and excessive attention to market timing and short-term performance strategies as but one aspect of the more fundamental problems in corporate finance and management. While we address them, we do not believe they can be wholly cured. Speculation, and even bubbles, have been a continuing part of financial markets too long for us to believe that a simple wave of the legislative wand can dispel them. But even if there were a magical wand capable of such extraordinary changes, our basic concerns would still remain. **Additional measures to raise the cost of transactions across the board, to discourage financial innovation, or to limit price movements, are unlikely to do much to improve patterns of trading and management.**[*]

What needs to be addressed are the mechanisms through which corporate management is selected, rewarded, and monitored. To whom are managers responsible? How are they held accountable for long-term performance? It has long been accepted that the owners of American firms have seldom played a sufficiently constructive role in corporate governance. Their holdings have historically been small and dispersed, limiting their ability to express their discontent with management; the only tool they had was the much noted "Wall Street Rule," through which approval and disapproval of a firm's decisions are displayed through purchases and sales of shares. But because no single shareholder had much influence, owners behaved collectively as "free riders," remaining

---

[*] *Horace J. DePodwin* comments that certain additional reforms of trading practices are needed. In particular, margin requirements in future and spot markets should be equalized. Both markets have forged unifying trading ties; whatever the margin requirements are, they should be the same for both markets.

dismayingly passive. They left the responsibility to someone else; alas, for the market as a whole, there was no one else.

In recent years, however, there has been increasing concentration of ownership by institutional investors, notably the pension funds. Institutions as a group now own more than half of the nation's total equities, up from one-third in 1980, and pension funds alone soon will own one-third of total equities. But despite the growing importance of their holdings, these institutions have not become more involved in the ongoing oversight of the underlying businesses. Most portfolio managers follow the so-called active strategies, which reflect a continuing emphasis on sector timing, asset allocations among an extraordinary and changing array of investment vehicles and securities, and a variety of similar tactics. Other funds have instead become "passive" investors, indexing their equity portfolios; buying five hundred, one thousand, or even more stocks in a predetermined basket that, at low cost, mimics the movement of the market as a whole. Active or passive, the focus has not been on businesses as such, but on the market. Beat it (the actives) or join it (the passives).

Owners should know the companies they have a stake in, and they should have, as our present-day institutional investors do not have, sufficient incentive, information, and influence to participate constructively. **Indeed, the members of the Task Force believe that capitalism without interested and effective capitalists is an absurdity, one that invites governmental intrusion. We believe that the most workable policy is one of "relational investing," in which the major shareholders, from industry itself or from among the institutional fiduciaries, are encouraged to take larger positions, in far fewer portfolio companies, and to hold them for much longer periods of time.** We think that shareholder monitoring is a necessary check, not just on the excessive executive compensation that has currently attracted so much attention, but on the more fundamental issues of the uses of capital and managerial competence.

Many have suggested that the answer to the riddle of corporate governance lies in more direct participation by shareholders through the proxy process. Others support relaxing procedural requirements and standards of proof for derivative lawsuits so that courts of law can be a vibrant forum for corporate oversight. Still others urge a strengthened role for outside directors, giving them separate advisers and specific mandates to supervise management more closely. Such reforms have already had some success, but these directions for reform seem to offer only modest additional benefits. This sort of activism may look good; while going down it may even taste good; but we believe that it may be as much symbol as substance.

The Task Force endorses some elements of the drive for greater corporate democracy (and relational investing by fiduciaries may be seen as a form of corporate democracy), but we reject the notion that the adversarial patterns of shareholder/management dealings that have grown up with takeovers should be strengthened. We endorse a corporate democracy involving an enhanced role in corporate governance for the sophisticated investor; however, we do not embrace a system that provides easy and inexpensive access to the proxy process by any shareholder, regardless of knowledge or goals. Full disclosure, another element of corporate democracy, does serve an important function. Indeed, in certain areas, such as executive compensation, additional disclosure should be required. Many of the restrictions on communication among shareholders are anachronistic and should be eliminated. But shareholder activism today tends to focus, as it must, on matters of formal procedures, such as the bylaws, or the symptoms of a corporate malaise, such as compensation. Neither constant shareholder confrontation with management nor more litigation is likely to contribute much to productivity or even to managerial accountability.

The Task Force recommends encouraging ownership by individuals and institutions that hold a few firms as a significant part of their portfolios, that see their future in the growing stream of income produced by these businesses, and that only indirectly, if at all, pay attention to short-term financial movements. The relationships cultivated by Berkshire Hathaway with Coca-Cola, GEICO, Washington Post, Salomon Brothers, and Wells Fargo are a good example. Berkshire holds positions large enough to be important to the corporation and also to the investor. The holdings at GEICO and Washington Post go back over fifteen years; all of them are said to be permanent. Annual reports make the difference clear. A typical institutional investor reports on the market performance of its portfolio relative to the major indexes. Berkshire's report discusses the business prospects and management of its affiliated companies. Without wanting investment funds to abandon diversification, and with no illusion that every fund will become a Berkshire Hathaway, **we believe that changes in the regulatory and tax environment, combined with changes internal to investment intermediaries, can make relational investing more attractive and more accessible.**[*]

---

[*] *Martin J. Rabinowitz* believes that the legal and structural limitations on pension funds make it virtually impossible for them to function in the same manner as Berkshire Hathaway. They can participate in similar relational investing through investment funds that specialize in holding substantial equity positions for the long term.

Relational investing implies a greater degree of shareholder involvement than many corporate managers might care to see. Not everyone wants a Big Brother. But **the Task Force believes that managers, small shareholders, and the public at large stand to gain by the participation of major and knowledgeable shareholders who can act as anchors in times of market turmoil or business adversity.***

Tax reform is needed both to facilitate relational investing and to increase the saving rate, thereby stretching the investment horizon by reducing the cost of capital.[†] Not only the capital gains tax but the tax treatment of interest and dividends must be changed. The goal of these reforms should be to encourage saving, to discourage speculation and to discourage purely tax-driven corporate restructuring.

---

[*] *James Grant*, while endorsing the value of relational investing, believes that in today's overvalued market it is not advisable for any investor to take substantial new positions for the long term. The implementation of greater relational investing should follow reforms that remove the distortions that result from the socialization of risk, brought on by federal subsidies of banks, bankers, bank lending, mortgages, and debt in general.

*Roland M. Machold* is pessimistic about the future of "relational investing" because of strong opposition by corporate managers to institutional investors over the years. Furthermore, he does not regard Berkshire Hathaway as a model and notes that some of its investments have been on favored terms and have put other shareholders at a disadvantage. Finally, concentration of holdings would not provide the advantages of diversification, which have been well documented. He does believe that investors should be able to combine their interests and retain professional intermediaries who could provide business expertise to companies as well as a friendly challenge when necessary.

[†] *Horace J. DePodwin* notes that today's capital costs—low by the standards of the past decade—are generated by the recession and cannot be expected to last.

*Benjamin M. Friedman* comments that skepticism is warranted regarding our ability to use the tax system to increase private saving. He points out that during the 1980s, the combination of lower tax rates, lower inflation rates, and higher market interest rates raised the after-tax real returns available to U.S. savers by a large multiple of what advocates of tax reduction and tax reform had argued would be sufficient to raise the U.S. private saving rate. Yet the saving rate fell anyway.

Our tax structure has aggravated some of the problems we seek to cure. By allowing a corporate income tax deduction for interest payments but not for dividends, the federal law helped to stimulate the debt explosion of the 1980s. By buying back one set of instruments (their stocks) and issuing another (notes and bonds), corporations could eliminate the government's share of the profits. Companies that announced a radical restructuring saw their share price leap by a third or more in a single day. That tilt toward debt has abated for the moment—held back by the sad examples of sound businesses unable to carry their self-imposed debt burdens through the recession—but the lesson is clear. Indeed, proposals to level the tax playing field for debt and equity are not new. It is time to act. **The Task Force believes that the corporate tax deductibility of interest should be eliminated and the corporate income tax rate should be reduced to eliminate the tax advantage of debt finance while maintaining revenue neutrality.**[*]

**We also recommend that the capital gains tax be steeply graduated, raising it on short-term gains while lowering it as holding periods lengthen.**[†] This particular tax change (again, far from a new idea) can, like the first, be designed to be revenue neutral. In addition to these two substantial tax revisions, others will be required to remove the disincentives to active participation in management by large owners.

In order to understand these policy proposals, it is necessary to consider how the financial and the real economies interact, in theory and in reality. [‡]

---

[*] *Richard F. Syron* agrees that debt and equity should be treated equally in corporate taxation, but he is somewhat concerned about the transitional impact of reducing the deductibility of interest costs. Mr. Syron is not sure that we understand, yet, the impact such a change might have on different industries. He would prefer to reduce or eliminate corporate taxes as part of an overall change in tax policy to emphasize consumption taxes and a reduction in the deficit.

[†] *C. Austin Fitts, Roland M. Machold,* and *Benjamin M. Friedman* dissent from the view that the tax on short-term capital gains should be raised.

*Martin J. Rabinowitz* comments that pension funds, some mutual funds and foreigners pay no taxes now on capital gains, so their behavior cannot be influenced by capital gains tax changes.

[‡] A recent research report for the Council on Competitiveness called *Capital Choices: Changing the Way America Invests in Industry*, by Harvard Business School professor Michael E. Porter analyzes many of these same issues.

12　◆　Who's Minding the Store?

## Financial Markets: Ideal and Real

While they cannot directly create wealth, financial markets are vital to those who build and run businesses. One need only look at the failures of socialism to recognize this. What investments should be undertaken? Which products should be produced? How? Without signals from markets—product and input prices, share prices, and interest rates—not even the wisest planner can find the answers. Financial markets are vital to the process that allocates resources over outputs, over technologies, and over time. They allow some to specialize in production while others specialize in managing risk. They intermediate between savers with surpluses and entrepreneurs with investment plans. That is why the signals coming from financial markets are so important.

Ideally, participants in financial markets would be well informed and judicious. They would evaluate information unmoved by the madness of crowds. The prices at which financial instruments settled would offer no arbitrage opportunities: asset prices would reflect accurately the present value of future earnings, adjusted for risk. There would be little reason for such prices to change often or widely. History gives us ample evidence that earnings streams, while far from invariant, are not volatile in the long run, nor are real interest rates. So one might expect asset prices to be relatively stable, too, sending a steady signal to managers and investors alike about the long-run prospects of various enterprises. A good innovation would be rewarded with increased asset value, even if it could not be expected to pay off for some time. Gimmicks and window dressing would be recognized as such: a fresh coat of paint would not unduly affect the value of a house; short-term reshuffling of an asset portfolio would fool no one about its fundamental soundness.

In this ideal world, managers of financial portfolios—wealthy individuals or, more importantly, managers of the institutional portfolios that today dominate financial markets—all would realize this, as would their employers. It would be obvious that corporate performance must, on average, be average. It would be obvious that frequent trading, in the absence of solid new information, would—on average, again—provide extra income to no one but brokers. It would be obvious that real income for asset owners has, in the long run, only one source: efficient real production. There would be every reason for financial markets to reward good managers and perspicacious investors and to penalize momentum investing and other market-timing techniques.

Managers of institutional portfolios would play another role as well. As their holdings became larger and larger, portfolio managers would realize that "the Wall Street Rule" no longer works. A huge pension fund simply cannot substantially restructure its portfolio unobtrusively and quickly, expecting to pass a "bad coin" to others. Large investors would realize, then, that they must take their role as owners more seriously. Rather than treating firms' production decisions as data and reacting to them with their trades, they would use their shares to influence the course of management. Regulatory structures would accommodate this behavior. So financial markets would send signals not only indirectly through prices but also directly through exercise of ownership rights and power.

Real world financial markets do not follow such textbook rules. Asset markets are far more volatile than theory predicts. In too many cases, they drop 10 percent or more in a few days without any significant new information. The history of bubbles is long, covering such mundane assets as company shares and real estate and such exotica as tulip bulbs. Manic expansions regularly precede panics. While markets are moving up, there is never a shortage of ingenious plans that will work, forever; when bubbles break, many experts confidently announce the end of good times, forever.

Financial management is driven by mercurial forces. The dictionary may define an investor as "an individual or organization who commits capital to become a partner of a business enterprise," but it is the rare portfolio manager who has the luxury of buying fundamentally good assets and holding them through thick and thin. Pension funds, for example, often hire a variety of fund managers, each of whom specializes in a different asset allocation strategy. Meanwhile, an array of consultants reports to large committees, quarter by quarter, recommending shifts in sector weighting. In this system, who dares to say which assets are fundamentally good in spite of poor short-run performance? What better signal is there of long-run prospects than quarterly movement in share prices? Any portfolio manager who cannot show results quickly is not doing his job.

Portfolio managers are under great pressure to produce above average results consistently, a feat that is mathematically impossible for them as a group. So they compete feverishly, always on the lookout for a shred of information that will give them an edge. Such information may be superficial—a fresh coat of paint, window dressing—but who is to know? As long as other traders in asset markets are playing by the same "rules," it behooves the competitive portfolio manager to see this as a signal of a short-term price movement. He ought to trade on it, if he is to produce the results expected of him. Even if a market participant believes that information about a firm is of no fundamental value, he should trade on it if he believes others will use the information to make their trades. Paradoxically, traders may disregard information they think is meaningful for long-run profits and instead use information they think is spurious, because they believe that other market participants are using the spurious information. The goal for a portfolio manager is to be right in the short run, if he wants to be around for the long run.

What is the significance of this for the shop floor? Does behavior in financial markets have any more importance for management of production than does the behavior of players in Las Vegas or Churchill Downs? Of course it does. **Chief Executive Officers and their teams are paid to produce results that will raise share prices. Only if share prices accurately reflect the present value and the risk of earnings may a manager concern himself with fundamentals alone.** If, as in the 1960s, markets heap large rewards on conglomerate acquisitions, managers will make indiscriminate acquisitions in order to capture those gains. If, as in the 1980s, markets heap rewards on firms that leverage to perilous levels by restructuring, management will heed these demands of the market or risk losing their jobs in a takeover. Managers strive to produce the results that financial markets value, and American managers do so more than others.

In corporate governance, too, the world does not match the theoretical ideal. Pressure for short-term performance, regulatory restraints, and force of tradition have greatly slowed the transition of institutional investors from passive to active ownership. As one money manager said, "we are not paid to be good citizens at General Motors." A few public and union pension funds have actively involved themselves in corporate governance; but many more have chosen instead the low cost route of purchasing indexed portfolios of stocks. If almost everyone buys and sells for short-run gain, or relies on others to play the role of investor, who is left to behave like the dictionary's "partner in a business enterprise?"

## POLICY

Debate over public policy measures to deal with our economic problems is active and contentious, but it is so unrelenting that the public rarely pays attention. Occasionally, an economic crisis will drive home our vulnerability: Unless the government intervenes, the stock market, or the banking system, or a firm too big to fail will capsize. Proposals for fundamental reform are debated, sometimes at the highest levels, but these usually drop quickly from public view as the conventional order returns to financial markets.

**The members of the Task Force believe that "business as usual" in financial markets is no longer acceptable. Whatever disagreements may persist about the value of one policy measure**

**or another, it is clear that our economy is not performing well enough to meet global challenges.** Therefore, we have put forth policy proposals in three broad areas.

First, we briefly consider policy to influence the character of trading activity itself. If the high volume of trading and short average holding periods characteristic of our financial markets reflect the short-term perspective of market participants, some have suggested, then perhaps measures to make such strategies more difficult or costly could push participants toward more investment-oriented, less gaming-oriented strategies. We are skeptical about the usefulness of such measures, however.

Second, we turn to the role of investors in corporate governance. Neither of the two major checks on management—the shareholders' right to elect directors and corporate takeovers—seems to be sufficiently effective. Even major institutional shareholders prefer to sell shares rather than to try to influence management. Here our system differs fundamentally from that of our main commercial rivals, Germany and Japan. In those countries, relationships between corporate managers and their principal financial and industrial investors are central to corporate governance. The question is, What can we learn from them?

Third, it is also necessary to consider broader measures that might affect the overall saving and investment performance of the economy. If we are to foster a long-term outlook by management, the cost of capital is vital because it measures the pressure to repay quickly. The saving rate in an economy helps to determine the new resources available for new investment, which, in turn, influences the real interest rate and the cost of capital. Tax law may, within limits, influence private saving decisions. Fiscal policy determines the public contribution to the saving aggregate. Together, these policy measures influence the cost and the volume of funds available to the private sector through financial markets.

## RECOMMENDATIONS CONCERNING TRADING

After the dramatic crash of the stock market in October 1987, a great deal of attention was focused on trading practices in financial markets. The Brady Commission as well as other analyses pointed to the plethora of instruments and opportunities that made it easy to take highly leveraged positions, at low cost, in multiple markets.

Complicated buying and selling strategies, such as portfolio insurance and other forms of program trading, also have received close scrutiny. These strategies, which often generate sell orders in a falling market and buy orders in a rising market, are based on the assumption that any one trader's decisions are insignificant compared to total market transactions.

**16** ◆ WHO'S MINDING THE STORE?

Even if this assumption usually is right, if many trades are driven by similar computer programs, their collective effect can be to destabilize the market, driving the price higher in a bull market and accelerating a price decline. Since there are no strong roots to hold it steady, the market valuation, which is the outcome of the mass psychology of short-term traders and programmers, is liable to change violently as a result of a sudden change of opinion that is barely connected to the prospective return on the underlying asset. Much of today's trading activity, particularly in new derivative instruments, is difficult to explain or to justify as more than gambling.*

We question whether our economy derives as much benefit as it should from the high transactions volume, the proliferation of instruments, and the billions devoted to supporting the equity trading establishment. To argue that current trading practices have met the test of the market is not sufficient defense. There are markets for all sorts of goods and services, socially destructive as well as socially desirable. The question is how much these vast resources are contributing to the real economy.

It is possible that measures to reduce directly the volume of trading and the maximum rate of price movement in a day or an hour will discourage high-turnover, gaming strategies by asset owners and managers. Nevertheless, **the members of the Task Force doubt that transaction taxes or additional circuit breakers will induce**

---

* *Muriel F. Siebert* notes that some of the trading practices described here, which contributed to the severity of the 1987 crash, have been moderated or are obsolete now. The creation of collars for trading halts in volatile markets today precludes a market free-fall similar to 1987. Such regulation was put into place in reaction to the 1987 crash. Other measures—such as the SOES (Small Order Execution System)—have helped increase fairness for smaller investors by insuring that their orders receive priority on the electronic execution systems. The most obvious problem that has not yet been addressed is that new derivatives and trading practices are being created regularly. Regulation has just not kept pace with these developments. It is imperative that a global regulatory framework or network be created—either by markets privately or by governments—to monitor these developments so that we will never have a similar event.

*Roland M. Machold* believes that derivatives are mechanisms that legitimately help investors balance their risk and reward prospects more effectively.

**a longer-term outlook in financial markets.** Transactions taxes are too easily evaded in globalized financial markets.* It also is unlikely that more circuit breakers would accomplish much.

As noted earlier, the Task Force does endorse one measure to discourage high-turnover, short-horizon trading. **The capital gains tax should be graduated, falling dramatically as the holding period lengthens.** Thus the capital gains tax on an asset held for less than a year should exceed that on an asset held for a few years, which should exceed that on an asset held for many years. Although some long-term considerations may lead an owner to hold an asset only briefly, and some speculators who are unconcerned with fundamental value may hold assets longer, on balance we believe that **a steeply declining capital gains tax will discourage a short-term outlook, at least by market participants whose incomes are taxable**. (In order not to impose a corresponding penalty for longer-term capital losses, these taxes could be offset against capital gains even of a shorter duration.) A graduated capital gains tax also will compensate for some effects of inflation on asset values. The divergence between nominal and real capital gains is much greater for an asset held for years than for one held only for weeks. The lower tax rate on the asset held longer reduces the penalty of inflation.

Such a change in the capital gains tax should not be confused with an across-the-board tax cut. The reform can be revenue neutral—with the tax rate raised at short holding periods, when turnover is rapid, and lowered at the other end—or it can be formulated to increase or decrease the average capital gains tax rate. The revenue implications of the capital gains tax reform should be planned together with overall budgetary policy.

## Recommendations Concerning Corporate Governance

**The Task Force believes that "short-termism" should be countered primarily through reform in the practice and regulation of corporate governance.**

In principle, the managers of corporations are employed by boards of directors, who in turn are accountable to the owners—that is, the shareholders. Many observers agree that there are serious problems with the current arrangement. A common complaint is that corporate executives may run their own ships tightly, but when they serve as directors elsewhere, they become lax. Neither is shareholder involvement through the selection of directors a credible check on management. If a group of shareholders is dissatisfied with the directors' oversight of management, and tries to obtain representation, it must traverse a mine field

---

* *James Tobin's* dissenting opinion is appended to this Report.

of hazards to wage a proxy battle, even if it controls a considerable block of shares. In practice, a full-fledged proxy fight rarely occurs.

Incentives for long-term planning provided by the threat of wholesale change through a corporate takeover or leveraged buyout also do not do the job. Although it was hoped that the threat would force managements to exploit their firms' assets fully, even if directors provided little direction, takeovers in the 1980s were as likely to target companies that were well managed as those that were not. Worse, the process systematically came to depend on speculative levels of debt that often wounded bidder and target alike. In leveraged buyouts, managers themselves took advantage of market mispricing of assets to make windfall gains at shareholders' expense through management buyouts, reflecting the fact that the management group no longer regarded itself even remotely as the custodian of shareholders' interests.

Public policy on hostile takeovers has been ambivalent, to say the least. Hostile takeovers threaten not only entrenched management but established jobs, tax bases, and other benefits to various constituencies. Barriers to hostile takeovers may be popular among those threatened by change, but they further reduce the accountability of management. **The Task Force thus opposes measures such as multiconstituency legislation that have the ostensible purpose of making management accountable to the community and other stakeholders but have the actual effect of making it accountable to no one. Instead of policy to separate management from owners, we would like to see expanded direct oversight of management by owners, including major individual investors and fiduciaries.**

The most popular approach to increasing owner oversight of management, as mentioned earlier, is through greater corporate democracy. Policy to promote this goal includes such measures as easier access to shareholder lists, the elimination of barriers to communication among investor groups, and, more radically, free access to the management proxy statement for full-fledged proxy contests by groups owning as little as 3 percent of the shares.

There is much we support in the corporate democracy movement but we want to draw attention to two potentially serious problems. Too often, the push for corporate democracy posits and encourages an adversarial relationship between management and ownership. In such an "us-against-them" world, owners, at best, hold management accountable. This reduces the likelihood that the overseers will be a source of useful advice for management or that information will flow freely between them. Second, greater corporate democracy can open the door to efforts by fringe groups and individuals to tie up corporate resources in proxy battles. In seeking to pry open the proxy process, the shareholder rights movement at times seems indifferent to whether power passes to a professional corporate raider, a major pension fund, an investment bank, or a sophisticated private long-term investor. **The Task Force believes that it is essential to develop corporate democracy in a way that encourages relational investing, with collaboration and a continuing dialogue between management, major owners, and financial backers. A proliferation of proxy fights and legal battles between management and owners will do little to improve management practices.**

We believe that it would be valuable to reserve seats on boards of directors for directors who are nominated as elected representatives of sophisticated shareholders and to enable such shareholders easier access to each other. But more fundamental relief from our management problems may be found in the institutional arrangements in Germany and Japan, as well as historical experience with merchant banking in this country. We would like to see financial and corporate intermediaries, as well as sophisticated individual investors, take substantial ownership positions in enterprises and use these positions to work directly with managers to promote long-run competitiveness.

Of course, international and historical models must be modified by the unique features of modern American capitalism. No one would wish to leave the door open to abuses of power by a handful of holding companies. And to the extent that a merchant banking model weakens the "fire walls" between enterprises and financial intermediaries, it is important to retain safeguards that protect the integrity of the finance and payments systems in the event of failures in the nonfinancial sector; nonfinancial companies should not be allowed to control banks. Finally, it is important to recognize the role that non-bank financial intermediaries— especially pension funds, insurance companies, and mutual funds—might play in this country. These caveats notwithstanding, **the Task Force believes that regulation should be reformed to facilitate greater active participation by sophisticated investors (defined much as similar terms have been defined by the Securities and Exchange Commission) in the companies they own.**

To strengthen the relationship between large owners and management, a number of regulatory changes are necessary. Financial intermediaries—mutual and pension funds, banks, and insurance companies in particular—must be permitted, indeed encouraged, to take an active role as owners. It is likely that regulation will need to be tailored to the various intermediaries. A study of rules governing pension fund management should precede regulatory reform in this area. **The Task Force believes that SEC restraints on communication among shareholders should be relaxed, as the commission itself has just approved. Accounting rules, too, must be reformed to allow greater flexibility in the level of cross-corporate stock holdings (restrictions on equity method accounting presently penalize an intermediary that acquires more than a small interest in a firm). Tax law must remove the penalty on these holdings that, by imposing an additional layer of income tax, turns what would otherwise be an acceptable rate of return into one that is demonstrably inadequate.**

The Task Force expects that in a restructured regulatory environment, new institutional investors will arise or existing mutual funds will modify themselves to become active long-term shareholders in a limited number of companies. With restrictions relaxed—on ownership levels, active participation, and communication among investors—such holding companies could pursue their self-interest by exerting constructive pressure on management.

Regardless of the means adopted to permit large owners to participate in corporate governance, these owners will play the constructive role we urge upon them only if they, too, change. As long as fiduciaries' financial officers are themselves monitored almost continuously, as long as they are expected to hold portfolios that are not just diversified but are spread thinly over hundreds of assets, as long as portfolio managers are expected only to sell and buy rather than to attempt to influence management, regulatory reform to enable more active ownership by financial intermediaries will bring few concrete changes.

**Money managers must be evaluated on the basis of their performances over a longer run.** It is likely that the biggest intermediaries will continue to take the lead in establishing an active role in corporate governance. Their very size limits their opportunities to play only by the "Wall Street Rule." Managers must learn to accept that sophisticated investors are not troublesome outsiders but resources to be used. If American managers can gain from long-term relationships with their financial backers, as is the case in Germany and Japan, then we all stand to gain. The skills and minds devoted to financial analysis should be contributing more to the real economy than they do today.[*]

---

[*] *Horace J. DePodwin* believes that it is important to recognize and applaud actions by a number of boards of directors of major U.S. corporations that have recently—albeit late in the game—moved to improve their governance. Additional comments by Mr. DePodwin are appended to this Report.

REPORT OF THE TASK FORCE ◆ 21

## RECOMMENDATIONS CONCERNING SAVING AND INVESTMENT

If one is concerned about the long run, nothing is more important than saving for productive investment; without it, capital will be scarce, real interest rates will be high, and the investment horizon will contract: "short-termism." Investment in capital, people, and ideas is the fundamental source of economic growth. Small differences in growth rates compound into substantial differences in standard of living. History demonstrates how quickly a slow-growing world leader can become a secondary power.

It is difficult for the government to change private saving behavior. But the taxation of income from capital is an area in which reform could encourage private saving and investment. Here, too much attention has been focused on reducing capital gains taxes. An across-the-board reduction of the capital gains tax rate will serve up windfall gains on past investments that already have been undertaken. And it will create no direct incentive to lengthen the investment horizon. What is more, the preoccupation with capital gains has led to neglect of discussion of the taxation of net earnings and interest. At present, tax law encourages corporate leveraging by exempting corporate interest costs from taxes while it taxes dividends twice, first as corporate income and again as personal income.

**The Task Force believes that more than reform of capital gains taxes is needed. We need comprehensive reform of taxation of income from capital. The principal element in such a reform is the equal tax treatment of debt and equity.** Reform of taxation of income from capital not only would reduce disincentives toward saving and investment but also would reduce the incentive to engage in socially useless corporate restructuring that simply exploits differences in the tax treatment of debt and equity.

More equal treatment of debt and equity can be approached in various ways. The least radical proposal would simply reduce the corporate income tax rate, and remove the deductibility of corporate interest costs. Revenue neutrality can be achieved by adjusting the corporate income tax rate applied to earnings.

## CONCLUDING COMMENTS

It is clear that the 1990s will be very different from the 1980s in financial markets. We know now that it is harder to promote growth than to make financial deals. Our energy and creativity must be redirected to ensure that the resources involved in finance contribute more to the real economy. Productive real investment depends on the laws, regulations, and the very culture and attitudes that direct the attention of savers, owners, managers, and bankers to the long-run consequences of their actions. Financial markets, left to themselves, will not efficiently care for the long term. We need both public and private policy reform to marshal the resources in our financial markets to contribute more to our international competitiveness.

## DISSENT

by James Tobin

I welcome the recognition by this Task Force, with its expert and diversified membership, that managers of U.S. corporations are excessively concerned with short-term results, registered in the market prices of their securities, and that those financial market prices themselves are often poor guides for managerial decisions, because securities investors are too much swayed by transient news and too little focused on fundamental long-term values. I can believe that the recommended reorientations of corporate governance and of institutional investors' behavior would be beneficial. What is not so clear is how government policies can bring about the desired structural, attitudinal, and cultural changes. The suggested reforms of regulation and taxation work in the right directions. But they seem insufficient to effect the "relational investing" revolution.

Partly for this reason, I think the Task Force was wrong to give such short shrift to "sand in the wheels" of the financial markets. A transactions tax could reinforce the Task Force's recommendations relating capital gains tax rates to holding periods. In the sentence in which the Report dismisses the transactions tax, ease of evasion "in globalized financial markets" is the reason given. Yet with U.S. leadership, the G-7 might coordinate this and other policies. And, with some ingenuity, it should be possible to collect these taxes from transactors themselves, to the extent they were not collected in the markets where and when the exchanges took place.

## COMMENT

### by Horace J. DePodwin

Institutional conditions and practices affect corporate governance and encourage speculation in ways not fully covered by the Task Force Report. Hence, these comments are intended to point out some additional areas where reforms may be needed.

The most important conditions include one noted in the Report: the long-standing tax conventions that burden equity more heavily than debt. Debt is favored, also, by governmental limits on equity held by investment trusts. Such limits, which are sometimes set by political rather than economic criteria, generally cover equities by amount and type. These conditions enlarge the volume of both long- and short-term corporate debt and provide an incentive for leveraged buyouts. Correcting the bias that favors debt should retard the erosion of the nation's corporate tax base.

A second set of institutional conditions and practices involves the tendency of many investors to sell securities rather than resist management actions adverse to their interests. A related problem is that independent shareowners are disadvantaged in takeovers (relative to insiders). These practices entrench managers and their boards and impair the financial and ownership claims of independent owners. Leveraged buyouts by insiders are encouraged and efforts to maximize short-run value at the expense of long-run returns may be encouraged as well. In addition, all too many directors lack independence from top executives, which only stimulates management to pursue its own interests at the expense of investors.

Accounting conventions for financial disclosure after acquisitions do not require historical income statements and per-share data to reflect the separate performances of the acquired and acquiring companies before the purchase. Consequently, the combined figures that are provided under current rules may allow an acquired company's superior performance to obscure the inferior past performance of the acquirer. When full information on the surviving firm's management performance is not evident, the firm may be able to raise capital more cheaply than it should, misallocating society's financial resources.

The third category of institutional conditions concerns securities and credit regulations that discourage institutional investors from acting together, and create risks for shareowners who oppose management. In addition, poison pill and state anti-takeover laws discourage buyouts and may insulate inferior managements and boards from market forces. To the extent that shareowners interests are compromised, society's resources are misallocated.

# Who's Minding the Store?

BACKGROUND PAPER BY

ROBERT J. SHILLER

# Introduction

Financial speculation—the buying or selling of financial assets with the hope of profiting from subsequent price changes—often seems to take a form that creates economic problems. Speculative behavior creates problems when it is destabilizing (that is, when it causes price movements that lack any valid economic rationale) and when it is excessive (that is, distracts attention from genuine economic decisions that should be made). If investors think that other investors will bid up or down the price of an asset in the short term, or if they think that other investors think that other investors will do so, then the investors may actually do so immediately, even if there is no good or sensible reason for the price change. The price movements that are generated by such behavior have real effects; they introduce a seemingly costly and unnecessary element of randomness in all our lives, and distract us from dealing with other economic problems. Speculative price changes in corporate equity affect real investment decisions of firms; they can cause people to be hired and fired, and they can cause companies to be taken over and reconstructed. The origins of our periodic recessions and depressions seem to have something to do with destabilizing and excessive speculation.

Many of our government agencies as well as existing and proposed financial regulations were created to deal with such speculative behavior. Much of what our Securities and Exchange Commission, Commodities Futures Trading Commission, and Federal Reserve System were set up to do is to reduce costs imposed by such behavior. With the proliferation of new financial intermediaries and new kinds of securities, futures, options, and other derivative markets, and with the recent flurry of hostile takeovers of firms, the question continues to arise whether these instruments and activities fuel destabilizing speculation, and whether they should be further regulated or even allowed to exist.

Financial speculation, of course, fulfills an important economic function: it can be stabilizing—pushing prices toward their true economic value—rather than destabilizing. When speculators buy corporate shares and other assets that they think will appreciate in the future, and sell those that they think will depreciate, their actions tend to push today's prices toward those expected future values. When speculators are not too preoccupied with market behavior, they may tend to expect future values to be sensible (from fundamental economic considerations), and thus they may work toward creating a price today that is in accord with those considerations. Such speculators are providing a useful service to society, by collecting information about real economic values and causing prices to reflect this. Thus the question is not whether it is good to allow speculation at all, but whether it operates in an optimal manner and, ultimately, whether it takes a form that leads to serious economic costs that could be prevented by modest changes in national policy toward financial markets.

Excessive speculative behavior is widely seen as creating a bias toward "short-termism." Short-termism can afflict both investors in shares of corporations as well as the managers and directors of corporations, so that none of these is mindful of the threats to the the long-term viability of the corporations.

When their interest in speculation is excessive, investors tend to hold shares only for a very short while, and thus they do not take the time to familiarize themselves with the true long-run prospects of the companies they invest in. They do not attempt to influence the operations of the companies they own, and provide no discipline on the managements of these companies.

The effect of such destabilizing and excessive speculative behavior on the managers and directors of companies whose shares are traded is to encourage them to be excessively concerned with appearances—with the likely market response to their decisions, rather than with the long-run wisdom of these decisions. This is especially true when business managers' bonuses are tied to short-run performance of the shares in their company, so they have a strong incentive to concern themselves with the behavior of the market. Then, management spends a great deal of time worrying about the next quarterly earnings report—time that may crowd out any attention to issues of the long-run profitability of the company.

When the term "short-termism" is used to refer to such problems, this suggests that these problems are tied up with the tendency of firms to underinvest—particularly in projects whose payoffs will occur in the distant future. It also suggests that the problem of short-termism may be related to inadequate national savings: inadequate funds made available to firms to invest, or excessively high cost of capital or discount rate faced by firms. But the basic problem alluded to by the term "short-termism" is not necessarily just a problem of inadequate levels of long-term investment as conventionally measured; rather it is a lack of genuine long-term investment. The problem is short term in the sense that errors in management are the kind that won't be discovered except in the long term. We are talking here about management's sweeping problems under the rug and pretending they are not there—not management's announcing that it will not deal with long-term problems.

The concern with speculation-induced short-termism is an important and legitimate one, not only in light of economic theory but also in its association with such broader potential problems as inadequate national savings and the high cost of capital. But at the same time, we need to be careful not to implement new policies and regulations that compromise the useful benefits provided to society by speculators. In the following pages I will try to put these concerns in perspective and assess proposed policy measures that might help improve the functioning of our financial markets.

Chapter One

# Speculation and Market Volatility

On October 19, 1987, the day of the worst one-day stock market drop in history, the Dow Jones Industrial Average fell 16.5 percent in two hours and forty-five minutes, from 2081 at 1:15 P.M. to 1738 at the 4:00 P.M. EDT closing. There is no sensible explanation for this dramatic price drop. No news of any conceivable significance to the nation's corporations broke during those hours, and there is no good economic reason why the nation's corporate equity should have lost nearly a sixth of its value in less than three hours.

None of the major studies of the stock market crash attempt to make economic sense of what happened in those hours. Often, the studies concentrate on reactions to news breaks that came days before. For example, the studies have emphasized October 14 news about the trade deficit or the House Ways and Means Committee's proposals for taxation of mergers. While these studies give evidence that suggests that these news events affected stock prices when the news broke,[1] they do not explain why such an enormous reaction to the news breaks did not occur until five days later, between 1:15 P.M. and 4:00 P.M., on October 19, 1987.

Certainly, reactions to economic news take time to develop; investors need time to think over the consequences of news. Nonetheless, it is extremely unlikely that investors around the country would all come to their decisions at the same time. Unless they were massively using the electronic news media during those hours to reach a decision—say, discussing the news and offering major analyses right then—there is no way that they would reach a sudden consensus. Large numbers of traders simply have no means of reaching quick decisions together; they communicate with each other only through their effects on price and volume of trade in the financial markets.

Now, there is a longstanding impression among many observers that markets are basically "efficient" and that we should assume financial price movements have a sensible cause (efficient-markets theories will be discussed at some length below). This impression is widespread among many academics in finance. It is common, too, among journalists who write about financial markets. News media commonly try to give a sensible story that accounts for stock price movements, attributing stock price movements to new data about indicators of economic growth, to new announcements by the Federal Reserve, or to new tax initiatives in Congress. But during those hours on October 19, 1987, there was no such news, nor was any new consensus reached about the meaning of recent news. People were not directly reacting to news breaks in those hours; they were observing and reacting to the actions of each other, through price and volume of trade.

There is no evidence that there was any appreciable change in people's expected discount rates or in expected corporate profits between the time just before the crash and just after it. A survey by Hoey, Rolley and Hotchkiss of institutional investment managers in September 1987 showed that the expected pretax real bond yield was 4.00 percent; in November 1987, their survey showed this expected yield had *declined* to 3.71 percent; this decline in the real rate of discount would suggest a *rise* in the stock market, not a crash.[2] The Blue Chip Economic Indicators, a survey of fifty-one professional forecasters, showed that in the first three working days of October 1987, immediately before the crash, pretax profits (current dollars) were expected to grow 7.1 percent during the five years 1988–92 and 7.3 percent during 1993–97. In their first post-crash long-range projection survey, conducted in the first three days of March 1988, pretax profits were expected to grow 7.0 percent during 1990–94 and 7.5 percent during 1995–99. (In the March 1988 survey, pretax profits were expected to grow 2.9 percent in 1988 and 5.9 percent in 1989.)[3] These profits forecasts do not show any substantial decline in the outlook for profits at the time of the crash.

Efficient-markets theorists, aware that there was no apparent reason for the crash on October 19, have tried to argue that the price movements themselves might carry information about what was in the minds of investors. Gerard Gennotte and Hayne Leland, as well as Charles Jacklin, Allan W. Kleidon, and Paul Pfleiderer, drawing on earlier work of Sanford J.

Grossman, have argued that the price drops on October 19, 1987, might have been due to investors inferring something adverse about market liquidity from the price drops themselves.[4] A simplified argument along these lines would be that initial price drops, due to some small news events, were perceived by investors as more than expected (based on their previous impressions of the likely response of the market to such news events). If investors underestimated the amount of stop-loss or portfolio-insurance selling, they might have thought that the October 19 price drops reflected a decline in market liquidity, and such a decline might have represented a good reason to sell. But why should market liquidity have been dramatically lower in October 1987? Gennotte and Leland argue that a decline in liquidity might have come about if there are relatively few "informed investors"—but they offer no confirming evidence (or any reason to suspect) that there was any decline in the number of informed investors.

Thus, these efficient-markets theories successfully explain how we *might conceivably* reconcile the crash with efficient-markets models, but they offer no empirical evidence that would support their interpretation over other interpretations. In effect, the changes they attribute to a decline in "liquidity" might be just due to market psychology. In my own questionnaire survey, conducted just after the October 1987 crash, investors were asked to give their interpretation of the crash in their own words. Most of them categorized their theories as having to do with market psychology, and their explanations seemed much more primal and less calculating than would be suggested by the efficient-markets models.[5]

Although there are a number of special considerations to take into account regarding October 19, 1987, it appears that what happened on that day is old-fashioned speculative panic. People began to fear that, because of the fears of other investors, stock prices would crash, and in effect they created a crash in their efforts to get out of the market.

## THE SIGNIFICANCE OF EXCESS SPECULATION

The stock market crash of 1987 is a pretty clear example that price changes can come about in the absence of any good economic reason. On a normal day, when price changes are much smaller, there is usually no way to judge whether a price change is a rational reaction to news events of the day. But the 1987 crash suggests that the market has a life of its own, even on normal days.

Speculation-induced price changes need not necessarily be only price drops. The other side of speculation is the price run-ups that occur when people begin to think that future price rises are likely, and thus

36 ◆ WHO'S MINDING THE STORE?

start to buy. A vicious circle can then proceed in an upward direction, with price increases spurring more price increases and again and again. Speculative price changes are not necessarily confined to price changes in the aggregate stock market either; groups of stocks that investors view as related may show dramatic speculative price changes apart from the market as a whole. And, of course, speculation may occur in a wide variety of other markets: bond markets, commodity markets, real estate markets, and collectibles.

The sudden price change that occurred in the U.S. stock market on October 19, 1987, represented major changes in economic decisions, affecting the long-run plans of the corporations whose stock is traded on the exchanges. The drop in price between 1:15 P.M. and 4:00 P.M. had a direct impact on the ability of these corporations to finance new investments: the market would make something like 16.5 percent less money available to companies in exchange for new issues of their stock, and hence 16.5 percent less of an opportunity for these companies to invest by equity issue in new plant and equipment, in research and development, or market penetration. And yet, clearly, no information about the long-run profitability of the companies was responsible for this change in price. In this sense, some short-term speculative considerations had an impact on the long-term decisions of our corporations.

The kind of costs of speculation that we see in the stock market are found in other markets as well. The market for real estate provides an example of these costs that is familiar to most of us. The housing and land market has shown a tendency to go into occasional booms, followed by periods of slack demand and sagging prices; these phenomena cannot always be explained in terms of fundamentals such as population movements or business conditions.[6]

During a real estate boom, for example, people who had planned to buy a house in the future begin to worry that if they wait they will not be able to afford to do so; they may buy sooner than they wanted to, thereby fueling the boom. During a real estate boom, young single people may buy and occupy houses suitable for large families—houses that are more a burden than a pleasure for them—just to make sure that they will have a house later. At the same time, somewhat poorer families with children, who might have been able to afford these houses had there not been a real estate boom, remain in cramped quarters. Builders then have an incentive to overbuild the housing stock, since the price of housing becomes high relative to construction costs, thus widening their profit margins. Later, after the boom is over, there may be too much housing for the long-term demand, and we may again see people owning and occupying houses that they do not want—holding on in the hope that there will be a pickup in demand (and in price). The market psychology after the boom may then contribute to a business recession as well.

## SHORT-TERMISM AND SPECULATION

Many characterizations of speculative behavior, even on the part of investment professionals, include a claim that the behavior is in some sense short term in objectives or motives. In 1936, John M. Keynes made the point that "the actual, private object of most skilled investment today is to 'beat the gun. . . .' This battle of wits to anticipate the basis of conventional wisdom a few months hence, rather than the prospective yield of an investment over a long term of years, does not even require gulls among the public to feed the maws of the professional; it can be played by professionals amongst themselves."[7]

Speculators, however, need not have a short-term focus, as was noted over fifty years ago by Benjamin Graham and David L. Dodd:

> An investment authority on common stocks has recently defined an investment [versus speculation] as any purchase made with the intention of holding it for a year or longer; but this definition is admittedly suggested by its convenience rather than its penetration. The inexactness of this suggested rule is shown by the circumstance that *short-term investment* is a well-established practice. *Long-term speculation* is equally well established as a rueful fact (when the purchaser holds on hoping to make up a loss), and it is also carried on to some extent as an intentional undertaking.[8]

Still, it is perhaps the case that much speculation is concentrated on relatively short-term trading, and the use of the term "short-termism" to refer to speculation has had a long history.

The sense in which speculative behavior involves "short-term" biases in thinking may be that speculators, who are by definition concerned with price changes, are concerned with changes in market valuations of the long stream of future cash flows that an asset is claim to, rather than with changes in the long stream of cash flows itself; since price is the valuation at a point of time of a claim on this long stream, the former changes are of shorter time span than the latter.

This short-termism on the part of investors, this tendency of investors to be concerned with price changes, rather than with changes in the long stream of cash flows, means that there is an incentive for the managers of firms whose shares are traded to play up to or even fool the market.

So long as the managers of firms whose shares are traded benefit from an increase in share price, there will be a short-term bias in management activities. Short-termism on the part of managers is a tendency to manage so as to look good to the market; that is, to do what investors think other investors want, to deceive investors about the outlook for the future cash flows of the company and to undertake activities that look good to such investors even if the activities reduce the outlook for such cash flows.[9] This notion of investor and managerial short-termism does not necessarily imply any tendency for managers of firms whose shares are traded to tend to spend too little on investment in the future of the business on the whole; they may even tend to make too many long-term investments if the making of these investments fools investors in such a way as to boost today's price. But this is still short-term behavior on the part of the managers, since it will be discovered to be bad behavior in the longer term. The bad effects of speculation are related to the short-term in the sense that they are due to an "information gap" between investors and managers—a gap that necessarily disappears in the long-term when cash flows are revealed.[10]

Concern about speculation or "short-termism" in our financial markets has been expressed countless times over the past few years, both in the United States and in other countries. This concern is so widely expressed because evidence of destabilizing speculation is so easily found in everyday life. But it is less easy to know how the government and business sector ought to deal with such speculation, and how to formulate policies that are in the best national interest.

Chapter Two

# Recent Concerns and Policy Proposals

C oncern about the problems caused by financial speculation is hardly new. Thomas Jefferson, in a 1787 letter to George Washington, wrote that "the wealth acquired by speculation and plunder is fugacious in its nature and fills society with the spirit of gambling." Theodore Roosevelt, in his message to Congress on January 31, 1908, said that "there is no moral difference between gambling at cards or in lotteries or on the race track and gambling in the stock market. One method is just as pernicious to the body politic as the other kind and in degree the evil worked is far greater."

In the past decade, a great deal of attention has been focused on the speculative behavior of institutional investors, rather than individual investors. Institutional investors are professionals who manage large investment portfolios representing such things as pensions, trusts, endowments, or insurance reserves. Recent concerns about speculation have taken on a new form and new sense of urgency, however, in reaction to changes in financial markets:

▲ Senator Lloyd Bentsen, chairman of the Senate Finance Committee said: "I'm deeply concerned about the churning of stocks and short-term horizons. That's been particularly true of the pension managers and some of the tax-free funds."[1]

▲ Felix Rohatyn wrote in a *Wall Street Journal* op-ed piece: "The fundamental weakness in the securities markets, world-wide, is the result of excessive speculation, excessive use of credit, and inadequate regulation. This speculative behavior is not driven by individuals, as it was in the 1920's, but by such institutions as pension funds, banks, savings and loans, and insurance companies."[2]

▲ Senator Nancy Kassebaum wrote in a *New York Times* article: "At the Senate Banking Committee's recent hearings on industrial productivity, the witnesses included an impressive array of investment bankers, economists, and corporate leaders. Their assessment was urgent and unequivocal: We must 'lengthen' institutional investors' short-term mentality. Otherwise, we face the prospect of losing our status as a major industrial power."[3]

A bill to reduce speculation, S.1654, introduced by Senator Kassebaum, the Excessive Churning and Speculation Act of 1989, deals with certain institutional investors: employer pension plans. This would impose a tax on the short-term capital gains of pension-fund portfolios, currently untaxed, to discourage them from trying to make short-term trading profits—that is, to discourage them from speculating. Although this 1989 bill is now dead, the content of the bill still has substantial support, and similar provisions are likely to be considered with the next capital gains tax initiative in Congress.

One reason why the speculative behavior of institutional investors is perceived as causing special problems is the alertness of such investors to new trends and their ability to move large sums of money around very quickly. Institutional investors today use computers to enable them to buy or sell large baskets of stocks simultaneously. They now also have computer-generated trading strategies, which may cause automatic purchases or sales to be made. One widely cited factor in the stock market crash of 1987 was the "portfolio insurance" programs that caused a lot of automatic sales of baskets of stocks on that day.

Associated with the rise of institutional investors and the increased professionalization of financial management has been the development of a variety of derivative financial products: futures on stock price indexes, options on index futures, options on actuals, and other synthetic equities traded over the counter. The stock index futures market was initiated in the United States in 1982. Since then, the volume of trade on the Standard and Poor's 500 stock index contract has been at times greater than that of the New York Stock Exchange itself. These derivative products make new kinds of speculative strategies possible or make it cheaper to undertake some old strategies, and some think that because of the speculative activities they encourage, new regulations should be imposed to discourage these markets:

▲ Louis Lowenstein testified before a congressional committee that: "Futures Markets are worse than useless. They distort the process by which capital markets are supposed to allocate resources to their most productive uses. They divert attention from the business fundamentals that are the market's proper concern."[4]

▲ James Tobin wrote: "The country cannot afford all the markets that enthusiasts may dream up."[5]

While the complete abolition of financial futures markets is an extreme proposal, a number of proposals that are more likely to be instituted would hamper these markets.

The 1980s have seen a major takeover movement. Companies whose equity is perceived as underpriced by certain large institutions may find themselves bought out by these institutions, which may then make major changes in the structure of the company. Associated with these takeovers is often an enormous swing in the price of the shares in the target company, and shareholders and potential investors in the target company may find themselves more concerned with the potential for these price movements than with the underlying business of the company. Many states have enacted anti-takeover laws that would discourage such "speculative" activity.

The Pennsylvania anti-takeover law was enacted in 1990, during a control battle between Armstrong Industries and the Belzberg group. Proponents of the law cited concern about the kind of disruption successful takeovers might cause on the lives of employees, communities, and other interests. The bill was, in fact, promoted as a measure to deal with the very "short-termism" that we discuss here. The *New York Times* quoted Steven H. Wallman, a lawyer at the Washington, D.C., firm of Covington and Burling, who drafted the bill, as saying: "We've seen our country go from a major world power to the now-now-ism of a short-term orientation. . . . The Pennsylvania vote shows we want to go back to that long-term view."[6]

The alleged problems of short-termism and speculation are also tied up in many people's minds with other problems in our society. Policy measures aimed at these might also have an impact on speculative behavior.

For example, associated with the recent concern about speculation and with financial deals has been a recent concern about a decline in the "work ethic" in the United States. People are concerned about a decline in commitment to do a good job in one's everyday occupation, about a rise in expectations among Americans that wealth should come easily, an increased admiration of dealmakers and salesmen rather than producers.[7] There is no evidence, though, that people are getting lazy;[8] in fact, people are thought to be more competitive and are putting themselves under increasing pressure to work hard. But such competitive tendencies do not necessarily correspond to tendencies to admire people who feel a commitment to doing ordinary jobs well.

According to William McGowan, an observer of social trends: "While a less forgiving economic climate gives people obvious incentives to work harder and be more focused in their careers, the pressures of tighter times also put a gun to the head, denying the necessary slack to make moves where the return isn't readily apparent or guaranteed. . . the machinery we have set up to test competitive abilities also encourages early and empty achievement devoid of long-term payback for society as a whole."[9]

There is also a recent concern about a decline in ethical standards. The Boesky scandal and the Milken scandal call to mind the range of similar scandals that took place in the 1920s speculative boom. These news stories suggest a decline in a sense of the importance of trust in business dealings over the past decade. The recent buyouts of corporations financed with junk bonds involved some abrogation of trust to various stakeholders in the corporations. Preexisting bondholders were hurt when the quality rating of their bonds dropped sharply. Some employees who had been led to believe that the company would try to provide job security to them felt that implicit contracts had been abrogated.

The savings and loan crisis (the recent insolvency of many federally insured savings and loan associations, and the consequent need for the federal government to pay depositors at these insolvent institutions) is often taken as further evidence of a decline in ethics. When savings and loan associations were deregulated, allowing them to pay high rates of interest to attract deposits, there was inadequate policing of their investments, and many savings and loans pursued a high-risk investment/high deposit interest rate strategy.

The more conservative savings and loans could no longer compete for deposits when others offered such high deposit interest rates, and so many managers of savings and loans found that they had either to quit or to emulate the same strategy. Business standards fell widely, and in some cases so far that some savings and loan managements committed outright fraud.

I will not attempt here to deal with all of these apparent ills of society, but will concentrate instead on the problems directly associated with financial speculation, and the policy measures aimed directly at these. Doing just this is not easy, however, as there is no substantial agreement on how we should think about speculation.

## Chapter Three

# Speculation and Economic Theory

Concerns about speculation-induced price movements are generally motivated by what may be called behavioral theories of financial markets. Behavioral theories describe the origins of price movements in terms of patterns of human behavior, such as tendencies toward gambling or tendencies to adopt current fashions.

Standing in diametric opposition to the behavioral theories is the efficient-markets theory of financial markets. According to this theory, when financial assets are traded on competitive markets, their prices accurately reflect all public information about the intrinsic value of the asset—and nothing else. In other words, to quote one major textbook in finance, "every security's price equals its investment value at all times."[1] This theory might be described as saying that we needn't look at any patterns of human behavior as resulting in price movements, since people do nothing else but rationally use all information to find the best possible investments for themselves.

Both of these theories have a wide following. In this chapter, I will examine these theories for the elements of truth in each. I will argue that both behavioral and efficient-markets theories have some merit; neither is adequate by itself to explain the behavior of financial markets. Then I will discuss the implications of speculative behavior on prices—in particular, the tendency for price "bubbles" to occur. A bubble is a protracted increase in speculative prices, but an increase that, by its very nature, cannot be sustained indefinitely; the bubble must eventually burst.

46 ◆ WHO'S MINDING THE STORE?

There are both rational bubbles and behavioral bubbles; the latter mediated by faddish behavior, focal points, and popular models. Finally, I will discuss what this all means for the ability of financial markets to allocate resources effectively.

## BEHAVIORAL THEORIES OF FINANCIAL MARKETS

Many behavioral theories of financial markets include the following elements: the tendency toward gambling behavior, the tendency to be overly influenced by current fashions and fads, the tendency toward overconfidence in one's own abilities and good luck, and the tendency to apply attention irregularly.

Gambling behavior is a psychological phenomenon that is found in all cultures, all walks of life. According to a Survey Research Center study of gambling in the United States,[2] 61 percent of the adult population placed some kind of bet in 1974; 48 percent placed bets on one or more commercial form of gambling. Of those who placed bets, the average total wager in 1974 was $387, or about $1,000 in today's prices. The study concluded that 1.1 percent of men and 0.5 percent of women are probably "compulsive gamblers," who have so much trouble controlling the gambling impulse that they experience difficulties managing their lives. Although these are small percentages of the entire population, it is likely that a much higher fraction of the population shares some of the characteristics of compulsive gamblers.

Gamblers tend not to be simply "risk lovers," who like to take chances. They tend to develop an ego involvement in a particular form of gambling. They tend to think either that they are expert in playing that game or that they have a winning hand or string of luck in that game. Playing that particular game is often described by gamblers as yielding a sort of "high," an aroused and pleasurable sensation that chases away their cares, a high that can even be addictive.

In gambling behavior, there is often too much of a belief in the uniqueness of events occurring at the present time, too much of a tendency to assume that a run of good luck will continue, too much of a tendency to disregard sobering evidence. This is essentially the error that many have alluded to who note that Graham and Dodd's classic advocacy of long-term investment is the "most widely read, and most widely ignored" book.[3] The error in thinking that simple comparisons with past statistics are irrelevant and that the present offers unique opportunities is not exactly an error in self control, as some suggest. Because there is true uncertainty, the behavior in any one instance is not clearly an error at all, and the gambling aspect of behavior may play a role here only in pushing people to an action amid uncertainty (more on true uncertainty below). Even someone who is very intelligent may sell on the day of a stock market crash because of his or her emotions, given that there is no objective reason not to sell.

A tendency to "follow the crowd" and adopt opinions that are currently in vogue among one's associates has been studied extensively by sociologists. Of course, people do not just believe anything that they hear others around them expressing, but there are well-confirmed biases in judgment that social psychologists have identified through experiments. Consider the classic experiment of Sherif on the "autokinetic effect."[4] Subjects in this experiment were placed in a totally darkened room and asked to watch a point of light emitted from a small box to judge its movements: they were to report to the experimenter the direction and magnitude, in inches, of its movements. In fact, the light was not moving at all—although this was hard to verify—since there was no frame of reference in the total darkness with which to judge its position. If subjects were placed in groups so that they could hear each other's answers, the individuals tended to arrive, without discussion, at consensuses on the amount of movement. The consensuses differed across groups. When subjects were interviewed afterward, they usually showed little awareness of the influence of the group on their own answers.

Because of extensive interaction with each other and through opinion leaders in the media, large numbers of investors may tend to think similarly, so that their actions do not tend to average out across investors and hence they have a market impact. Word-of-mouth diffusion of opinions among investors may also cause a classic "epidemic" of opinion change, like those of contagious diseases. The dynamics of the spread of investing attitudes may resemble those of the spread of a disease if attitudes are spread primarily from individual to individual. Social psychologists have found that "any impact that the mass media have on opinion change is less than that produced by informal face-to-face communication of the person with his primary groups, his family, his friends, coworkers and neighbors."[5] Indeed, this fact has long been recognized by television advertisers, who commonly try to give the impression (using actors) of such peer communication.

Overconfidence, a tendency to feel in control of circumstances or to feel that one's own knowledge is superior to that of others, has been often remarked in the psychological literature.[6] One often gets the impression, in talking with investors, of overconfidence in their own opinions, though it is, of course, hard to judge the validity of these impressions.

In a recent survey prepared for the New York Stock Exchange by Dean Witter Financial Services Group and A. G. Edwards & Sons,[7] shareowners were asked how strongly they agreed with the statement: "If you study companies carefully you can pick a winner in the stock market." Of the five hundred respondents, 18 percent strongly agreed, 42 percent agreed somewhat, 21 percent disagreed somewhat, 15 percent disagreed strongly, and 4 percent had no opinion.[8] The 18 percent who strongly agreed may have a substantial effect on market prices; certainly the 60 percent who agree at least somewhat can. This was a survey of individuals, not investment professionals, but there is no reason to think that pension officers are completely different.

In a survey that I did of both wealthy individual and institutional investors just after the stock market crash of 1987, I asked investors: "Did you think at any point on October 19, 1987, that you had a pretty good idea when a rebound was to occur?" Of the individual investors, 29 percent said "yes"; of the institutional investors, 28 percent said "yes." While this percentage represents a minority of investors, it is a very substantial minority—far larger than the percent of investors who trade on any given day or week—and these people are capable of influencing the market very substantially.

Certainly, there was no scientific or objective basis for an opinion on October 19, 1987, as to when the rebound would occur. The day was one of a record price drop, for which there were no historical precedents. From the respondents' written explanations of their thinking on the questionnaire, it appears that they were guessing the course of future prices based on intuitive theories of price continuation or reversal or on the psychology of other investors—hardly theories that ought to inspire great confidence.

Lapses of attention are another problem that afflict decisionmaking even of very intelligent people. The history of human achievement is one of great successes when attention is lavished on narrow areas of endeavor, and at the same time a history of opportunities overlooked. Thus, obvious important considerations for investment professionals may long be overlooked—for example, accounting properly for defined-benefit pension obligations or diversifying one's portfolio abroad. Factors that had once been overlooked may suddenly be appreciated, and may even lead to an investment fad.

The effect of all these judgment errors on market prices need not work primarily through the actual commission of the errors. Rather, given this behavior, investors may think that others will make the errors. For example, one might well give in to a gambler's impulse to sell on the day of a stock market crash because of a quite rational suspicion that others are feeling the same impulse. Or, one might sell then because one thinks that others will suspect that others will sell on the impulse.

## The Efficient-Markets Theory

The financial markets exist as a capital-allocation mechanism: they stand between the providers of investment funds (the savers) and the users of investment dollars (the corporations that invest in their business the money they obtain from new issues). According to efficient-markets theory, the stock market functions as a place where everyone's information about opportunities for investment, both short term and long term, is optimally pooled, resulting in optimal prices of financial assets and an optimal allocation of investment dollars: dollars are funneled to the corporations that can best use them in building factories, expanding operations, and so on. The allocation, moreover, comes at the time when the corporations can best use the funds.

According to the efficient-markets theory, any price movements, such as those at the time of the stock market crash of 1987, must therefore be due to some sensible news about economic fundamentals. There is a good reason why every price is where it is, and there are no bargains in the stock market. Under the efficient-markets hypothesis, there is no point in trying to pick stocks that are good values and that will perform well. One might as well throw darts at the financial page to select which investments to buy and which to sell. According to this hypothesis, there is no point in trying to time when to go in or out of the market. One might as well come into or pull out of the stock market whenever it strikes one's fancy to do so. Moreover, if markets are truly efficient, it is impossible as well to do systematically badly with one's investments, by picking the wrong investments or by coming into the market at the wrong time; for if one could do that, then one could also do well by doing the opposite, and that would contradict the efficient-markets hypothesis. Thus, there is no need to protect naive investors from their ignorance, so long as they are trading on competitive markets.

The term "efficient markets" was first popularized in the 1960s,[9] but the concept that markets ought to be efficient has a history that may be as long as the history of concern with speculation. Over a hundred years ago, George Gibson wrote that when "shares become publicly known in an open market, the value which they acquire there may be regarded as the judgment of the best intelligence concerning them."[10] The tension

50 ◆ WHO'S MINDING THE STORE?

between this view, as enunciated by Gibson, and the alternative view that speculative behavior influences financial markets, has continued for over a century.

Over fifty years ago, John T. Flynn, a prominent U.S. journalist and economic adviser, vigorously denounced this efficient-markets view: "The argument assumes that professional speculators make expert studies of the financial condition and earning powers of corporations and with this as a guide put a price on stocks which price the market follows. Of course, this assumption is utterly without foundation. . . . These men give little thought to the financial condition or earnings of corporations. They are concerned wholly with one problem—Will someone be willing to pay a point or two or three more tomorrow or the next day or next week or next month for the shares which they propose to buy today? The determining factors in the problem are credit conditions, market psychology, the general situation, good publicity, and, in many cases, the state of operations being carried on in the shares by insiders. Thus, prices are fixed without any reference whatever to actual investment values. And the speculative values which control the price fixing are concerned not with the long term growth possibilities of the underlying business, but with the short term gyrations of the prices."[11]

Why, despite the evidence that speculation and psychology influence financial markets—which was so convincing to Flynn and others—has the efficient-markets hypothesis appealed to so many? There are several, interrelated arguments for the efficient-markets hypothesis. These arguments are of some merit and do indeed suggest that some *very approximate* version of the efficient-markets theory holds, although they do not rule out that price movements are primarily speculative.

The simplest argument for market efficiency is based on the observation that there is a lot of smart money. Wall Street professionals are seeking bargains in the financial markets. These professionals should have the effect of bidding up the prices of underpriced assets. Within minutes of the time that some good news becomes public, some of these professionals will buy, perhaps until price increases eliminate the incentive to do so. Moreover, they can sell or short assets after bad news, tending to bring asset prices back down rapidly to their true investment value after the news. There is certainly an element of truth to this argument for efficient-markets theory.

But how much could these "smart money" traders influence the market? The answer depends on the amount of wealth that these traders have to invest (as well as the elasticity of demand of other investors). If one's impression is that the amount of wealth in the hands of smart money is very large, then one might well conclude that the efficient-markets hypothesis ought to be a fairly accurate description of what goes on in financial markets. If one's impression is that there is relatively little smart money, then one might conclude that the smart money may not have enough influence over market prices to make them efficient.

There is an argument that smart money may tend to become more influential over time, because smart money investors tend to make money and hence to accumulate wealth. The conclusion that many have drawn is that smart money will take over the stock market. This "survival of the fittest" argument certainly has some validity.

For example, suppose there were a profit opportunity that arose, let us say, thirty times a year and made 10 percent overnight for a person who invested in the right asset at the right time. Let us say, to elaborate, that the price of certain stocks tends to fall right after a certain kind of news break, because jumpy institutional investors overreact to the news break, creating a temporary bargain for a smart investor, and that the price always rebounds by 10 percent the next day. Someone with $1,000 to invest who became aware of this profit opportunity and on every occasion made the right investment would, if the profit opportunities kept arising, have $17,449 after one year, $304,481 after two years, $5,313,016 after three years, $1.6 billion in five years, and $2.6 quadrillion in ten years, which is vastly more than the entire world wealth. This vast wealth would accrue to anyone with any money at all who saw the profit opportunity, assuming such a profit opportunity was continually available.

Clearly, though, such a profit opportunity cannot persist; the investors' effect on price would eliminate the profit opportunity. Even if only one investor with very modest means becomes aware of the profit opportunity, that investor's wealth would become so big that the effect of his trading should work toward eliminating the profit opportunity.

While there is an element of truth to this argument for the efficient-markets theory, it does not support the claim that other kinds of profit opportunities that are less frequent or less reliable will be eliminated. Suppose, for example, that it were a fact in 1986—a fact that a number of smart money investors were able to perceive—that the junk-bond-financed takeover attempts bid prices up too high and that failure of these deals would likely occur in a few years. Here, the smart money will have little tendency to eliminate the price discrepancy. The smart money could arrange, by short sales, to profit ultimately from the crash in the junk-bond market, but they would have to wait years for this to happen. The timing of the crash is not such a sure thing that they could leverage themselves dramatically to take great advantage of this knowledge.

Another argument in support of the efficient-markets theory is based on the assertion that a large empirical literature has found that it is difficult to predict price changes (or, better, abnormal returns, properly defined) on speculative assets. It is true that many studies have not been able to find a forecastable component of price changes or abnormal returns, and earlier interpretations of the literature concluded that no substantial evidence against market efficiency had been found.[12] Given this, there is apparently some element of partial truth to this argument for the efficient-markets hypothesis.

Now, however, there are many studies that have found that returns appear to be forecastable. I, as well as Stephen LeRoy and Richard Porter, found evidence that stock prices are so volatile relative to fundamentals that returns must be forecastable.[13] Werner DeBondt and Richard Thaler found that stocks that did abnormally poorly in the past tend to do well subsequently, and those that did abnormally well in the past tend to do relatively poorly subsequently.[14] James M. Poterba and Lawrence H. Summers found that the variance of returns increases too slowly relative to the implications of efficient-markets models as the period of time over which returns are measured is increased, thereby suggesting that some "mean reversion" and forecastability exists in stock market returns.[15] Eugene F. Fama and Kenneth R. French found that while short-period returns are not very forecastable, long-horizon returns (measured over years rather than days or months) are substantially forecastable.[16] These studies, while widely acknowledged, remain somewhat controversial.[17]

There is enough truth to the arguments for efficient-markets theory to give it some value for policy analysis. We might refer to the theory, for example, if there were a bill in Congress that would ask the SEC or another government agency to try to stabilize the day-to-day movements in stocks, with the purpose, let us say, of preventing "jumpy" institutional investors from overreacting to news events on a short-term basis. We might argue, based on efficient-markets theory, that there would hardly be any point to this, since we can be pretty confident that smart money investors in the stock markets would already have eliminated such a major short-run profit opportunity. If the government *were* to attempt to stabilize stock prices by buying when the price was low and selling when the price was high, then the government would wind up doing the same thing that speculators are doing. The plus side of this is that the government should be able to make money by following this strategy. On the other hand, one might ask how the government can succeed in carrying out such a strategy, since any government employee who has the ability to carry out such a strategy has an incentive to quit and do it for himself.[18] These arguments against short-run government stabilization efforts, however, do not seem to extend to all efforts by government to reduce the probability of events like the stock market crash of 1987.

## RATIONAL BUBBLES

If all investors are very intelligent and rational and know that all investors are very intelligent and rational, could a speculative boom or crash occur? Efficient-markets theory, as usually interpreted, would seem to say no. Rational investors, knowing that other investors are rational, would conclude that a speculative boom or crash just cannot happen, and so they would do nothing to make it happen.

But if other investors do not behave in accordance with this expectation, then it may not be rational for any single investor to follow it either. If other investors are causing the market price to rise, then it will be rational for any given investor to buy too, and enjoy the profits of a price rise: the bubble grows. If other investors are about to make the market crash, then a given rational investor might be well advised to get out too, and might rationally do something—for example, sell—that contributes to a stock market crash: the bubble bursts. Since any given rational investor may be buying or selling for speculative reasons, why shouldn't one presume that all people who are rational and intelligent will do so?

This insight suggests the possibility of "rational bubbles."[19] Here, short-termism arises not because of anyone's shortsightedness, or anyone's stupidity, but because it is rational to behave thus, given that everyone else is behaving this way. Rational bubble models admit of multiple economic equilibriums: If everyone assumes that a crash can't happen, then it won't happen. That's one economic equilibrium. On the other hand, if everyone assumes a crash could happen on any day with a certain probability, and it does happen with that probability, then that is another economic equilibrium. Within each equilibrium, everyone is satisfied with his or her own way of behaving; given the consequences they observe of their behavior, they will not want to change it. Equilibrium, in this sense, does not mean that prices are stable—only that patterns of behavior are stable.

These rational bubble models confront a theoretical problem: How can periodic crashes be part of an economic equilibrium? If an investor knows that periodic crashes occur, and that the consequences are temporary, then can't he profit by trading differently—by working contrary to the crash when it occurs and buying when prices are low? Wouldn't this tend to eliminate the crash?

One way to salvage the basic notion of a rational bubble is to take account of the true uncertainty that characterizes the actual economy, and the limitations of intelligent behavior as we know it—that is, the inevitable limitations of even the brightest investors.

Frank Knight noted the importance for economic theory of the distinction between "risk" and "uncertainty."[20] According to Knight, one observes risk when one knows the probabilities and knows the relevant correlations. Risk can be dealt with systematically by pooling risks (insurance companies deal with risks on a systematic basis). With true uncertainty, on the other hand, according to Knight, there is no knowledge of—nor any way to find a group of similar instances from which to infer—probabilities or correlations with other events; the event under consideration seems to be unique. Knight wrote that "it is this true uncertainty which by preventing the theoretically perfect outworking of the tendencies of competition gives the characteristic form of 'enterprise' to economic organization as a whole and accounts for the peculiar income of the entrepreneur."[21]

An event like the stock market crash of 1987 may be considered unique. It was by far the biggest one-day drop in stock market history. It might be compared with the stock market crash of 1929, but so many things were different then that it is probably hopeless to try to learn from this earlier episode. Moreover, one is never sure whether smaller, day-to-day stock market movements should not also be considered unique; the economic environment is always changing, history always moves forward. Because those making economic decisions are faced with true uncertainty, even the best professionals find themselves guessing or relying on intuitive judgments, and they are capable of major error.

## Behavioral Bubbles: Feedback, Focal Points, and Popular Models

An alternative to the rational bubble model is a behavioral bubble model. The idea is essentially the same, but a behavioral bubble model relies on behavior that is not quite rational for everyone. Thus, an initial price increase in a speculative asset sometimes encourages some investors to think that such price increases will continue. Since we are dropping the notion that everyone is completely rational, the tendency of a bubble to grow depends on investors' variable tendencies to think this way. These investors may enter buy orders so that they can profit from the future price increases, thereby causing further price increases. These further price increases may encourage yet more investors into the market, and so on; a feedback loop—that is, a vicious circle—creates an upward trend in prices; the bubble grows. In a behavioral bubble, however, in contrast to a rational bubble model, the growth (and burst) of the bubble does not have an inexorable logic to it; it may pause for a while or fizzle, depending on the variable social behavior of people.

Booms and crashes do not happen every day, and so some conditions must be changing from time to time that make the feedback operative at some times and not at others. Speculative booms tend to occur only in periods when rising earnings or other indicators seem to confirm the feeling of optimism. Moreover, speculative booms are not characterized by a steady upward march of prices, as the rational bubble story describes. The upward path of prices during a speculative boom is not so easily distinguished from a realization of a random walk (where day-to-day price movements seem largely random up and down). There are nearly as many down days as up days during a "bull market." And speculative booms usually do not terminate in dramatic crashes.[22]

It is critical to understand that feedback of price increases to further price increases does not operate in a knee-jerk manner. People have theories or models of the economy; these popular theories and models change from time to time, causing the feedback mechanism to change. Moreover, people respond to many news events other than price changes—in ways that depend on the popular theories and models of the time.

Much of the seemingly erratic behavior of speculative markets seems to be tied up with news stories that might plausibly be interpreted as giving rational reasons for stock market movements. The stock market often moves sharply immediately after news breaks, and one is led to wonder, since the reaction to the news was so sharp, if the investors who set market prices might really know that the news is important to the future profits of corporations. But the importance of the news breaks does not seem to relate closely to the magnitude of the price movements.[23]

One example is illustrative. On Friday, October 13, 1989, the stock market took a major one-day drop. The drop came immediately after a news break: the announcement that a leveraged buyout deal for the UAL Corporation, the parent of United Airlines, had fallen through. Because the stock market drop appeared within minutes of this news break, it seemed highly likely that the news break was the trigger. But the UAL Corporation accounted for less than two-tenths of 1 percent of the value of the aggregate stock market, so it is hard to see how this one news break could rationally account for such a big market drop. Theories were expressed that the UAL news might have been interpreted by the market as a watershed event, which would be followed by failures of all attempted buyouts in the future. But these theories did not give any cogent reason why this little piece of bad news about buyouts should be interpreted as a watershed development.

William Feltus and I collected some evidence suggesting that the UAL news was not interpreted by the market as having any fundamental significance, but rather that the news was just a focal point on which other investors might have been presumed to wish to sell.[24] By a focal point, I mean just some event, even an irrelevant event, that might suggest that it is time for the market to move, and so it moves because people expect it to move. Imagine, by analogy, a game of tug-of-war, involving a large number of people, which has become stalemated: neither side is winning. The game may suddenly turn after something (say, someone shouts something) that suggests that others think it time to pull harder, or to give up.[25]

On October 16 and 17, 1989, we conducted 101 telephone interviews with investment professionals. We asked them:

> *Which of the following two statements better represents the view you held last Friday:*
>
> 1. *The UAL news of Friday afternoon will reduce future takeovers, and so the UAL news is a sensible reason for the sudden drop in stock prices.*
>
> 2. *The UAL news of Friday afternoon should be viewed as a focal point or attention grabber, which prompted investors to express their doubts about the stock market.*

Only 30 percent of the investment professionals picked "1"; 50 percent picked "2"; the rest had no opinion or gave no answer. Some further evidence on this matter is suggestive that the content of the news was not important. We asked:

> *Did you hear about the UAL news before you heard about the market drop on Friday afternoon, or did you hear about the UAL news later as an explanation for the drop in the stock market?*

Only 36 percent said they heard the news before the drop; 53 percent said they heard it later, as an explanation for the drop.

Why this news seemed a good focal point at that time is something that we do not understand; perhaps it had something to do with other recent news that had been received about takeovers, or perhaps it was due to the fact that October 13, 1989, was the Friday closest to the second anniversary of the tumultuous Friday before the stock market crash of October 19, 1987, or even to the fact that it was a Friday the 13th. But other anniversaries or Friday the 13ths have not been extremely eventful.[26]

In answering the question why the UAL news became a focal point, it is important to stress that it is not the content of the news that we should consider but the reaction that investors thought the market would have to the news. The reaction to the news is complicated and intellectual, and at the same time it is fundamentally speculative, and not to be understood in completely rational terms.

The popular theories and models that create an environment in which news events are selected as focal points are spread by word-of-mouth communications and investment media. The transmission of these theories and models may be slow, but communications and study by investors, especially investment professionals, are effective enough to cause changes in the broad pool of popular models and theories.[27]

Competition among the smart money investors tends to reduce the effects of popular theories or models, which might otherwise more dramatically affect prices (creating sharp profit opportunities), but leaves a transformed effect of these theories and models on market prices. According to one model, the smart money serves to make the market price a sort of present value expected by smart money of both future dividends and future demand by ordinary investors.[28]

## SHORT-TERMISM AND BEHAVIORAL BUBBLES

It was noted above that excessive speculation is not logically connected with a short-term outlook, but perhaps the tendency to equate excessive speculation with short-termism reflects some basic tendencies of human behavior. We have collected some information on such short-term tendencies.

In July 1989, Fumiko Kon-Ya, Yoshiro Tsutsui, and I sent questionnaires to four hundred institutional investors in the United States, to four hundred institutional investors in Japan, and to four hundred wealthy individual investors in the United States, asking them about their attitudes toward the stock market.[29] We sought, by asking questions about their investment strategies, to find out how they decide whether to hold stocks. They were asked to specify whether they have a speculative intent and what their trading horizons are. Specifically, the questionnaire asked:

*Although I expect a substantial drop in stock prices in the U.S. ultimately, I advise being relatively heavily invested in stocks for the time being because I think that prices are likely to rise for a while.*

58 ◆ WHO'S MINDING THE STORE?

*Circle one number; if you circle 1, also indicate date*

1.  *True. Your best guess for the date of peak:____/____/____*

2.  *False.*

3.  *No opinion.*

A substantial number of both individual and institutional investors answered "true" to this question, thereby indicating disbelief in the efficient-markets theory. Of the American institutional investors (154 respondents), 34 percent said true, (53 percent said no, and 13 percent had no opinion), while among individual investors (119 respondents), 44 percent said true (44 percent said no, and 13 percent had no opinion). (The sum exceeds 100 percent because of rounding.) Japanese institutional investors showed a similar tendency to think that people often were well advised to hold stocks only for the short term.

Those who answered "true" tended to make relatively short-term price forecasts. Of the American investors, both institutional and individual, who filled in their best guess for the date of the peak, two-thirds gave a date less than six months in the future; about 90 percent gave a date less than twelve months in the future.

Another question asked about price declines. The answers to this question revealed that an additional 25 percent of both individual and institutional American investors advised staying relatively less invested in stocks for the time being; these investors also tended strongly to think that the bottom of the market would come in less than a year.

These answers suggest that in July 1989, most investors were either relatively heavily in the market and thinking of reducing their holdings in the near future (hoping to exit before anticipated price drops) or were relatively lightly in the market and thinking of increasing their holdings after the market dropped. Although there was a strong difference of opinion among investors as to the direction of the market (recall our tug-of-war analogy above), there was relative consensus that the market ought to make its turn in the near future. The six- to twelve-month horizon for these anticipated moves was provided by the respondents, not suggested by our questions.

## SPECULATION AND RESOURCE ALLOCATION

What does the above discussion about speculative bubbles imply about the ability of our financial markets to allocate resources? It does not matter, essentially, whether the bubbles are basically rational or behavioral:

when the price of stock in a company or of another asset is raised artificially by a growing bubble, an incentive will be created for that company to expand its operations, and for others to try to create such assets; when the bubble bursts, that incentive is rudely retracted. Excessive speculation that creates such bubbles disrupts many business decisions.

The problems caused by such bubbles cannot be placed with speculators as a group, for there are speculators who have the opposite effect—that of smoothing prices and enforcing a rational basis for prices. To the extent that some speculators can see a bubble and its burst coming, these speculators may tend to short the asset while the bubble is growing, and buy it as it is crashing, therefore reducing the impact of the bubble.

On balance, one must concede that speculators as a group have a net positive social benefit, even if they regularly produce bubbles in prices. The effect of speculators on the stock market is analogous to that of a drunken airplane pilot on his passengers; we might blame most of the erratic movements of the airplane to his actions, but we would not want to let the airplane fly without him; it might fly smoothly to a crash. If we eliminated all speculation, then there would be no intertemporal consistency to financial prices, no one insuring that prices tomorrow bear any sensible relation to prices today. Thus, any policy that is designed to deal with the problem of speculative bubbles must be subtle, not eliminating speculation altogether, and not causing more harm than good.

To say that speculators have a net positive social benefit does not mean, however, that they are spending their efforts in a socially optimal manner. The amount of time and effort that speculators expend on the existing financial markets may be excessive from a broad social point of view.

A lot of speculators' attention and effort is devoted to trading shares in existing companies. In principle, the speculators who trade in these shares are directing investment resources to the most deserving companies. They have some tendency to bid up the price of shares in companies with good earnings prospects. Thus, good companies—that is, companies with good earnings prospects—are rewarded more with investment funds, while bad ones are penalized.

But companies with good dividend prospects are not necessarily the ones most deserving of new funds. An optimal allocation of resources would provide funds to companies with good current investment opportunities. But the price at which a company can sell new shares depends on the valuation given to its existing business, not just its contemplated investment plans.

If speculators collect information about the future earnings of an existing business, and if one day this information indicates that the outlook for future earnings has improved, then the price of the existing business will increase, and it will become easier for this company to raise funds for new investment projects. But what connection is there between information about the future earnings of an existing company and the wisdom of a new investment the company is contemplating? The connection can be very tenuous.

Consider a conglomerate that produces many different products but that is contemplating new investment in only one of these, or in something completely new. Possibly, the information that might lead to an increase in the price of a share in the company is about the quality of the company's management, which would extend to any new venture that management undertakes. But the information may also be about the demand for any of the other products that the company currently makes.

While it is true that the community of investment professionals does contribute substantially to the allocation of capital in this country, there is no reason to believe that the activities of this community are socially optimal for the country. The activities that they undertake might even consume more resources than the benefit that they provide. The most dramatic recent estimate of the resources consumed in financial speculation was made by Lawrence Summers and Victoria Summers, who estimated that the total cost of operating the U.S. securities market in 1987 was over \$75 billion, or one-fourth of total corporate profits and close to one-half of corporate net investment.[30] Bhide estimated that in 1986, stock-trading commissions amounted to 8.5 percent of the total earnings of public companies in that year; Lowenstein estimated that intermediaries revenues from trading might be as high as a sixth of corporate earnings.[31] It should be borne in mind, of course, that the activities of these investment professionals provide benefits other than optimal resource allocation for corporate investment; for example, these activities help people to maintain their savings in a liquid form with risks that match each individual's own preferences.

## Chapter Four

# Today's Concerns with Speculative Behavior

We have seen that concern that excessive speculation may be harmful is very old, even centuries old. Today, with changes in institutions, government regulations, and technology, that concern has taken on new forms. Many of the new concerns are due to the rise, in recent decades, of institutional investors—investors that may be too concerned with short-term investment results and with appearances. Institutional investors are thought to pay inadequate attention to investments for the long term, such as research and development; they are thought to overreact to short-term earnings announcements. The bureaucratization of investment management has been seen as causing a lack of creativity and insight—the corporate hierarchy as imposing a sort of "group-think" on investment decisions. Moreover, the rise of institutional investors means that the actual owners of assets, who might have a less short-term focus, are cut off from decisionmaking regarding these assets.

There are also other events, not directly tied to the rise of institutional investors, that have brought newfound concern with speculation. The flourishing of corporate takeovers in the 1980s has raised concerns that takeovers represent a new sort of investing fad that is especially disruptive to business activities. The proliferation of derivative financial markets and declines in the cost of trading since the early 1970s have brought concerns that it is now easier for excessive speculation to occur.

## INSTITUTIONAL INVESTORS AND SHORT-TERMISM

Professional investors are much more prominent in financial markets today than they were ten or twenty years ago. Institutional investors (pension funds, bank trusts, investment companies, insurance companies, foundations, and endowments) in the United States have been gradually acquiring increasing amounts of the outstanding shares of corporate equity. In 1981, institutional investors owned 39 percent of the total market value of equities; by 1986, they owned 43 percent, and they appear now to own about half of all the stock outstanding.[1] The same trend has been observed in other countries as well. In Japan, in 1980, 52 percent of all stocks were held by financial institutions (primarily insurance companies, banks, and trust banks); by 1987, this figure had risen to 61 percent.[2]

Associated with the increase in institutional investor participation in the markets has been a dramatic increase in the turnover of shares in our stock markets—a trend that has continued for many years. Turnover has more than doubled in both the United States and Japan since 1975.

It has often been asserted that the rise in institutional investors is responsible for the increased turnover. One piece of evidence often cited to support this claim is that block trading as a percentage of total trading volume has become quite high. Large block trades (trades of 10,000 shares or more) accounted for 54.5 percent of all shares traded on the New York Stock Exchange in 1988.[3] Louis Lowenstein argued that since these large block trades are almost exclusively made by institutions, and since small block trades (as small as 1,000 shares) are also made largely by institutions, institutions probably account for 75 percent of all trading—substantially more than the fraction of shares they own.[4] In Japan, disaggregated turnover data show that there has been an increase in the turnover rate of shares by households in the 1980s, but that more of the increase in aggregate stock market turnover is due to increased turnover among banks and business corporations.[5]

There are other ways of measuring trading activity besides simple turnover of individual stocks, and by these measures as well institutional investors are likely to be the more active traders. If one counts the volume of trade in derivative securities—index futures, options, and over-the-counter synthetic equities markets—then the increase in effective turnover of stocks would be more dramatic than the New York Stock Exchange turnover figures indicate.[6]

Why do many people think that institutional investors are to be singled out as the culprits responsible for speculative price movements? One might instead expect that the institutional investors would inject a note of greater professionalism into our financial markets and make things work better than if the markets were dominated by amateurs.

Apparently, one answer to this question is that the high turnover of institutional investor portfolios is taken as suggestive that they are more speculative than are individual investors. But the evidence is far from conclusive about the propensity to engage in speculative behavior. First of all, high turnover can come about because of the behavior of a minority of investors. Turnover rates in Japan are comparable to those in the United States, and yet there is in Japan a large group of very stable long-term institutional investors.[7] Turnover in Japan is made high only by a relatively small group of extremely active investors. Moreover, turnover can come about for a variety of reasons, including periodic reevaluation of long-term news or efforts to offset the speculative behavior of individual investors. The turnover among institutional investors might in fact represent the very kind of market stabilization activity that some concerned with short-termism might advocate that the government undertake.

A more important reason the institutional investor is accused of promoting speculative behavior is the common perception that institutional investors are subject to an incentive system that rewards shorter-term returns than are individuals, many of whom have very long-term horizons; many are planning for their retirement. There are also testimonials from institutional investors remarking on how short term the horizons of their colleagues are. But there does not appear to be any conclusive evidence that institutional investors are in fact ignoring the long-term profitability of the companies they invest in any more than did individual investors when they dominated the trade in the stock market.

Indeed, the effect of the rise of institutional investors might instead be expected to encourage more careful attention to the long run by managers themselves. This is because institutional investors are more professionally trained and more capable of systematically analyzing the forecasted future cash flows of corporations into the distant future. Their analysis can more accurately gauge the effects of future cash flows on the present value of the corporation.

## INSTITUTIONAL SHORT-TERMISM: IMPACT ON RESEARCH AND DEVELOPMENT

One form of "short-termism" allegedly induced by institutional speculative behavior is a bias toward neglecting research and development. The allegation, which has been repeated many times over the past five years, is nicely articulated by Senator Nancy Kassebaum, who claims that stock prices fall in reaction to announcements of increases in research in development:

> A case involving the Martin Marietta Corporation is a classic example. A few years ago, Martin Marietta announced an increase in spending on research and development. How did the money managers react to this apparently favorable news? They dumped their shares, fearing a possible reduction in short-term earnings. The company's stock price plummeted six points. Although Martin Marietta proceeded with the research program, its fortitude is rare. Fearing a negative institutional reaction, how many corporate managers would simply forego research and development?[8]

The same argument has been common in the United Kingdom. A recent editorial in the *Financial Times* described widespread "concerns among industrialists that short-term pressures from the City of London are damaging long-term investment in innovation."[9]

The staff of the Securities and Exchange Commission did a study to see whether such claims are valid.[10] Using the NEXIS news retrieval system for the years 1973 to 1983, they discovered sixty-two *Wall Street Journal* announcements that firms were embarking on research and development projects. Contrary to Kassebaum's assertion, there was an average abnormal return (a measure of price increase) of a *positive* 0.45 percent on the day of the announcement, followed by an additional 0.35 percent abnormal return the following day. These results have been given further support by other studies in the United States.[11] A similar study done by the Department of Trade and Industry in the United Kingdom (though hampered by the fact that far fewer announcements of research and development expenditures were found) also concluded that there was no observed tendency for stock prices to drop following such announcements.

The Securities and Exchange Commission study also found evidence that institutional investors as a group do not dislike research and development.[12] Their analysis indicates that, if one separates out industry effects, institutional investors tend to invest in firms with high research and development ratios. In a sample of 324 firms, 88 firms showed a decrease in institutional ownership from 1980 to 1983 and 236 showed an increase, yet there was virtually no difference in the research and development ratio for the two groups of firms. The study also found that in a sample of 57 takeover targets, the average research and development ratio was lower than in an industry control group, suggesting that embarking on a research and development program does not make a firm vulnerable to a takeover.

The Securities and Exchange Commission study and related studies provide impressive evidence that the bold claim made by Kassebaum is incorrect. It remains possible, however, that the general thrust of her argument about short-termism is correct. The basic notion that institutional investors have a short-term bias does not really impel us to the conclusion that they will react negatively to major announcements of research and development. If they are speculators, they will respond to major announcements by asking what these announcements mean for the demand for the stocks by other investors. Since major announcements are attention grabbers, institutional investors might well think that other investors will overreact to them in a positive way. Moreover, institutional investors who are speculators might react to data on research and development ratios by thinking that the market is overly positively impressed by these numbers. Lucian Arye Bebchuk and Lars Stole have argued that the bias induced on investments by short-term incentives depends on the nature of the information observed by market participants.[13] When investors cannot observe the level of investment in long-term projects, then there will tend not to be enough investment; when investors can observe investment but not its productivity, there will tend to be too much investment.

The essence of the argument that speculative behavior by investors can cause corporations to lose sight of their best long-term strategy is that in deciding how to react to an announcement or statistic issued by a company, an investor does not use his or her best judgment about what this means for the company, but rather a judgment about what other investors will conclude this means for price. It is plausible that investors will not attribute extreme naivete to other investors and will not assume that other investors will, for example, react in a reflexive negative manner to major announcements of new research and development initiatives. The game investors are playing against other investors is more subtle than that. It might instead mean that institutional investors will sometimes *not* react negatively to a research and development program that they know is misguided, just as often as they *will* react negatively to the announcement of a research and development program that, down deep, they suspect is a good one. In either case, the institutional investors' reactions may be inappropriate given actual import of the information for the long-term outlook for the firm.

As a means of looking for some truth in the assertions that such things as research and development that have an impact on short-run earnings may cause inappropriate movements in price, I mailed 400 questionnaires

## 66 ♦ Who's Minding the Store?

to institutional investors in the United States in January 1990, and received 140 responses.

I asked:

> *Do you think that the stock market tends to overreact to bad earnings news—i.e., that the market drops in reaction to bad news about short-run earnings, even when the bad news is not adverse for the present value of all future earnings?*
>
> *1. True                    2. False                    3. No opinion*

Of the 137 institutional investors who answered, an overwhelming majority—85 percent—marked "true"; only 7 percent marked "false"; 8 percent marked "no opinion." The high proportion marking "true" is especially striking given that the statement in the question runs sharply contrary to the efficient-markets doctrine taught in economics and finance departments of universities in recent years. I sought next, in a follow-up question, to find out if the investors trade on this opinion:

> *Do you base some of your buy-sell decisions on a theory of such market overreaction to earnings news?*
>
> *1. Yes, often          2. Yes, occasionally          3. Never*

Of the 138 respondents who answered this question, 14 percent marked "yes, often"; 73 percent marked "yes, occasionally"; and only 13 percent marked "never." Now, if most institutional investors make buy-sell decisions based on a theory that other investors will overreact to earnings news, this suggests that the market itself will in fact sometimes overreact to such earnings news. If the market did not overreact at all to earnings news, then the behavior of these institutional investors would make it overreact to such news. (It is still possible that these institutional investors surveyed largely offset the effects of individual investors who overreact.)

The institutional investors were more sure that the market overreacts to earnings than that the market reacts inappropriately to research and development expenditures:

> *Do you think that raising expenditures on research and development tends, other things equal, to have a negative effect on share price because of the effects on short-run earnings?*
>
> *1. True                    2. False                    3. No opinion*

Of the 136 institutional investors who answered this question, 33 percent marked "true"; 51 percent marked "false"; 16 percent had "no opinion."

Only a third answered "true" here, but this lower figure may just reflect awareness that announcements of research and development initiatives do not have a predictably negative effect on share price. The basic conclusion still is that institutional investors believe that "bad" news—even if only superficially bad—can be expected to harm stock prices, and that this belief ought to affect their trading behavior.

## SHORT-TERM PERFORMANCE PRESSURE
### ON INVESTMENT MANAGERS

Investment managers often complain that they are evaluated on too short term a basis—that they are not given adequate time to demonstrate their ability to manage their portfolios well. Some corporate clients of portfolio managers reportedly use the "12/24 rule," which is to fire any portfolio manager whose performance is 12 percent under the Standard and Poor 500 for any 24-month period. This rule certainly imposes some short-run discipline on a portfolio manager; the manager will find it difficult to accept any losses, even if the risk of losses is part of a sound long-term investment strategy.

The 12/24 rule is extreme because it imposes a severe penalty on losses. But investment managers are, in fact, often rewarded based on their short-term performance. According to a 1989 survey conducted for *Institutional Investor* magazine, of the 15 percent of pension funds that have explicit performance-fee arrangements with their portfolio managers, 45 percent use a one-year time frame in calculating performance fees, 4 percent use a two-year time frame, 41 percent use a three-to-five-year time frame, and 10 percent use another time frame.[14] A recent study of pension funds conducted by the Financial Executives Institute Committee on Investment of Employee Benefit Assets, suggests a slightly longer time frame:

> The survey [of] funds management of outside managers did not support the assertion that pension plan sponsors evaluate their managers primarily on short-term performance. The nearly unanimous response to the question relating to the time horizon over which managers are typically evaluated was "a three-to five year period" or "a complete market cycle." Moreover, the average tenure of managers currently employed by the surveyed funds is about 7.5 years. . . . Data indicated that managers are not "hired and fired" based on short-term pressures from plan

sponsors. In fact, the reasons given by sponsors for terminating investment managers were in addition to "poor performance" (1) a change in the fund's broad investment strategy; (2) changes in personnel; and (3) general decision to consolidate the number of managers.[15]

We might get better insight as to the pressures placed on investment managers from a more in-depth study of the patterns of thinking of those who hire and fire them. William O'Barr and John Conley, when they did an extensive interview study of pension fund officers, concluded that short-term pressures may be critically important in evaluations of investment managers, despite the fact that the officers who did the evaluations often claimed to have a longer-term investment horizon in conducting the evaluations. O'Barr and Conley's method, inspired by cultural anthropologists, was to encourage pension fund officers to talk freely about their concerns, listening carefully to the subjects that they raised and the words they used. "People are sometimes prisoners of their vocabularies," O'Barr and Conley concluded, and "the language of financial evaluation and accountability focusses almost exclusively on the short term. . . . Thus to focus seriously on the long-term is an act of intellectual originality that goes against the cultural grain."[16]

To get a better impression of investment managers' views on short-termism, I asked investment managers (as part of the January 1990 questionnaire survey described above):

> *Do you feel that your own accomplishments are properly evaluated by others who have influence over your career prospects with respect to your short-run investment performance?*
>
> *1. Short-run performance receives too much attention*
>
> *2. Short-run performance receives too little attention*
>
> *3. Neither or no opinion*

Of the 135 respondents who answered this question, 50 percent picked "short-run performance receives too much attention"; 4 percent picked "short-run performance receives too little attention"; and 46 percent picked "neither or no opinion." Those who felt that short-run performance receives too much attention outnumbered more than ten to one those who thought that it receives too little attention—though only half thought there was any bias in their evaluation.[17]

Of course, we cannot take these answers at face value as indicating that investment managers are given an incentive for a short-run bias in

TODAY'S CONCERNS WITH SPECULATIVE BEHAVIOR ◆ 69

their investments. The investment managers' complaint about too rapid judgment of their performance is a natural one for them to make; automobile drivers may complain that their auto insurance was canceled too quickly after just a couple of accidents (which may very well not have been the driver's fault), even though the insurance company may have been behaving properly from its viewpoint, not knowing more about the care with which its clients drive.

Perhaps a policy of, other things being equal, firing investment managers who do poorly in the short run is a useful benchmark to follow in judging portfolio managers. Those who employ investment managers presumably use this benchmark as just that—only a benchmark—and need not let it influence them unduly. Moreover, those who employ portfolio managers may be less concerned with "justice" in evaluating individual portfolio managers than in maximizing their own portfolio performance. If there are many competing investment managers, it may be good strategy to dump a manager who has done poorly in the past few years, as long as other managers who are equally capable are available.

It should be stressed that the use of a relatively short-term investment horizon to evaluate investment managers does not necessarily mean that the investment managers are being encouraged to take the short-term view (that is, neglecting longer-term investment potentials) in evaluating companies. The objective of the managers is to produce returns; any time interval provides some evidence of their ability to produce returns. Even if an investment manager is rewarded on as short a term as an annual basis, if the manager's own career objectives are long term, he or she will be concerned with the long-run average of his or her rewards—and this is the same as long-term investing. Taking the long view may be a paying proposition in the short run as well, since, on average, one would expect some long-run investment opportunities to bear fruit in a short-run period of evaluation.

The concern with short-term returns on investments may, in fact, tend to encourage long-term thinking. Consider the alternative, where there is no concern with short-term returns on investments; the institutional arrangement of state enterprises in the former Soviet Union is a good example. Profit incentives offered there reward those who run state enterprises who make good profits. But those who run state enterprises have no ability to sell shares in the enterprises, and therefore no financial stakes in the short-run changes in the value of the enterprises. These people have an incentive to destroy future earnings potential, which might have an immediate negative impact on the price of a share, were it traded, if it boosts short-term profits. The decline in future earnings

## 70 ♦ Who's Minding the Store?

potential may come after their own anticipated departure from the enterprise. Thus, for example, the manager of a Soviet enterprise who expects to leave his job in the next year or two may have little incentive to make any expenditures on preventative maintenance of plant and equipment. In comparison, an American manager planning to leave his job in that time might suffer immediately if share price declines anger stockholders. Certainly there is acute awareness of this problem today in the former Soviet Union, and this accounts for the substantial support for stock markets there. There is a felt need for short-term investment incentives.

The conclusion about short-term pressures on institutional investors is that such pressures can be a good thing; we do not want to eliminate them entirely. At the same time, the opinion among many institutional investors that short-term pressures are too great on them cannot be dismissed. Part of what concerns institutional investors may be a relative lack of enlightenment among those who choose investment managers as to the importance of short-term performance as a measure of managers' abilities.

## Judgment Errors of Those Who Choose Institutional Investors

A significant reason for a harmful bias toward short-term thinking among institutional investors is that clients do not understand how to judge the expertise of investment professionals. There is, in particular, a simple failure to understand how to use relatively short-term past performance statistics to evaluate investors' skills. By "relatively short-term" I mean using data on the past three or five years, or even more. The key issue that is not appreciated is that of selection bias. Since investment professionals use many different investment strategies, there will always be some that succeed just by chance. If we select investment managers who did well in the past, we don't want to make the error of assuming that their average past performance will carry over to the future.

The problem may lie with the people who *choose* investment managers, rather than with the managers themselves, who are investment professionals. Anise Wallace, a journalist who follows institutional investors, described the problems caused by those who choose investors based on their past performance:

> Many of the nation's supposedly sophisticated pension funds continue to pick their money managers by looking in a rear view

mirror. In a sheep-like herd, they rush to the "hot" firms of the moment, compounding their error by performing suspiciously like the most unsophisticated of investors. . . . "If I had to write a book about this business," shrugs one former money manager, "I would entitle it 'The Corporate Treasurer as Odd-Lotter.'"[18]

Moreover, the corporate treasurer or pension fund managers may be relatively enlightened next to the boards of directors who are often involved in pension decisions. According to one pension consultant, "Unless a pension officer has a strong hand in picking managers, he has to recommend the best recent performer. It's very hard to sell the board on a manager who isn't No. 1 out of a group of five."[19] Thus, institutional investors may themselves be professional, and not subject to short-term bias in their investments, but their clients, who are less likely to be investment professionals, may prevent them from performing optimally.

To explore whether this is so, my survey of investment managers included the following question, which immediately followed the question above about short-run performance:

*If you feel that you are not evaluated properly, who is ultimately more responsible for this error?*

*1. Members of your own firm        2. Clients of your firm*

Of the seventy-eight individuals who answered, 54 percent chose "clients of your firm," compared with 46 percent who chose "members of your own firm." There is certainly a feeling among institutional investors that clients of their fim share a large part of the blame for their short-term focus.

How good an indicator, then, is past success in predicting investment skill? Corporate executives and directors might naturally assume that past performance of investment managers predicts future performance just as well as past performance of production managers predicts their future performance. But investment managing may be different from other kinds of management, in that past performance does not count as much for predicted future performance. Until recently, it was common to summarize the literature as showing that the investment managers' past performance had no correlation with future performance. We now know that there is indeed a correlation; still, the element of chance makes the correlation a relatively weak one.[20] There is so much unpredictable noise in the market that chance alone has a great impact on outcomes of investment strategies.

All sorts of "success" stories can be generated if we allow the investor to be creative about the time interval chosen or sub-portfolio chosen for reporting. Institutional investors know this tactic very well. One controversial practice of mutual funds is to start many small "incubator funds." The new incubator fund is given a name (as part of a larger mutual fund institution), an investing approach or theory, and a small amount of money to invest. Afterward, by natural selection, the incubator funds that succeed will draw customers; the incubator funds that do not succeed can be forgotten. There is nothing dishonest about this strategy of mutual funds; they need not make false claims to customers, who will naturally move toward successful funds. The result is that investment theories or approaches that worked well just by chance in the past will tend to be given greater emphasis in the future—even if investment professionals themselves know that the success was only due to chance.

Of course, institutional investors still have an *incentive* to try to do sensible investing; other things being equal they will try to do a good job. The point is, though, that the quality managers will not be reliably rewarded with more money to invest; they will be lost in the pool of other "successful" money managers.

Institutional investors deal with an intelligent set of customers but not with a set of investment professionals. Mutual fund managers deal with the general public. Pension fund managers deal with corporate treasurers, boards of directors, and city and state government officials who are intelligent, successful people, but often unable to explain such basic investment concepts as present values. This is not a situation in which institutional investors who make the right "long-term" investments can expect to be singled out for their investment wisdom. Lacking a well-established, authoritative scientific community that would endorse an investment approach and evaluate an investment professional, there is no expectation that the good investment manager will be picked. Thus, investment managers complain that they are picked up or dumped for inadequate reasons.

To the extent that investment managers believe that they are evaluated by uninformed or naive people, they may be inclined to alter the management of their portfolios for appearance' sake—a phenomenon known in the trade as "window dressing." For example, window dressing may take the form of selling stocks that have done badly, so that they do not remain as reminders of past errors. According to journalist Nancy Belliveau:

The aspect of the problem most often cited by money managers is the growing pressure they feel to "window dress" their pension portfolios before each quarterly review session with a client. The source of this pressure, they say, is the abnormal obsession many corporate pension officers display toward short-term price fluctuations in the market. This shows up in the quarterly meetings, where the corporate men immediately focus in on the stocks that have dipped, to the exclusion of almost everything else. While admitting that such a review can, in its proper form, help a manager to face his mistakes, many managers feel that today it is often overdone—taking the form, one of them put it, of "a Chinese water torture." "The way it happens is very subtle," explains one long-suffering money manager. "For the fourth quarter in a row they'll say, 'Tell me again your feelings about those mobile home stocks. Do you still have your convictions? The damn things are so *unsightly* along the roads. . . . ' I finally cleaned out the whole bunch, because I got so damned tired of defending them."[21]

To get some impression of the prevalence of window dressing, I asked in my questionnaire of investment managers:

*Do you ever buy or sell a stock just for appearance' sake (window dressing)?*

*1. Yes                              2. No*

Of the 136 who responded, only 13 percent said "yes"; the rest said "no." The impression as to whether *others* do this, however, was very different:

*Do you think that many others tend to do this?*

*1. Yes                              2. No*

Of the 137 who responded, 61 percent said "yes"; 24 percent had "no opinion"; while only 15 percent said "no." While people were unwilling to admit to the practice themselves, there seemed to be recognition that window dressing does occur.

Window dressing sometimes goes beyond just selling losers. As revealed in my questionnaire of institutional investors, it also sometimes includes avoiding certain investments altogether:

*Do you sometimes not purchase a stock that you think is a good invest-
ment just because others have a prejudice against it and it would look
bad in your portfolio?*

*1. Yes*          *2. No*          *3. No opinion*

Of the 138 who answered, 28 percent said "yes"; 68 percent said "no"; 4 percent had "no opinion."

There appears to be a widespread belief that window dressing occurs. This belief may affect the demands for stocks even among those who do not window dress: They may buy or sell stocks in anticipation of the window-dressing behavior of others.

## INSTITUTIONAL SCLEROSIS

While institutional investors have greater training and more time and resources than individual investors, they may tend to do less well in investing: Sometimes decisions are made within organizations along bureaucratic or conventional lines that stifle creative thinking. Psychologist Irving Janis defined this problem as "groupthink" and provided a number of case studies of organizations in which experts made decisions that were so bad that it would seem that the man on the street should have known better.[22] In fact, in some of his case studies, members of the group harbored grave private doubts about their decisions, but they were inhibited from expressing these doubts in a group where social pressures inhibited them. Forecasts made within a professional organization may tend to have a conventional basis; one may be inhibited from raising doubts that are based on intuitive judgment if the conventional indicators that the group has decided to concentrate on are positive.

Just such a problem is thought by some to be the reason why the conglomerates of the 1960s failed to prosper. A central management over many disparate divisions may find that when conventional decision rules adopted by the management attain prominence, central managers may not be able to deal with subtle decision problems in the different subdivisions of their business.

The importance of such group-decision difficulties for institutional investors may be mitigated to some extent by the fact that their objective performance has always been observed on a regular basis; they are always getting feedback on the success of their investment strategies. But, of course, as was discussed above, the short-run immediate feedback on their quarterly investment performance may not awaken a bureaucracy to long-term strategic issues; there is room for "groupthink" problems to arise. Money managers' intuitive awareness of this social-psychological problem may account for their answer to the survey questionnaire noted above: that short-run performance receives too much attention.

## INSTITUTIONAL INVESTORS AND THE SEPARATION OF OWNERSHIP FROM CONTROL

The rise of institutional investors also corresponds to an increase in concentration of holdings of stocks: A corporation is more likely to have large stockholders who each own a substantial share of the company. This might then mean that managers are more likely to be disciplined by investors if they do not take proper account of long-term profitability.

Over a half century ago, Adolf A. Berle, Jr., and Gardiner C. Means argued that extremely low concentrations of stock holdings in large companies meant that the stockholders had in fact lost control over the management of their companies. When the largest stockholder owns no more than a few percent of the shares of a company, the stockholders are too dispersed to take any collective action. The control over corporations had shifted from the nominal owners to the managers of the corporations:

> The recognition that industry has come to be dominated by these economic autocrats must bring with it a realization of the hollowness of the familiar statement that economic enterprise in America is a matter of individual initiative. To the dozen or so men in control, there is room for such initiative. For the tens and even hundreds of thousands of workers, individual initiative no longer exists.[23]

In the absence of oversight by their shareholders, managers can engage in activities that have the appearance of good business but in fact have other motivations. When somebody else's money is at stake, an individual has a very different attitude toward spending: Managers may engage in corporate consumption, such as lavish offices and company jets. Also, any of a variety of distortions may enter their decisions, such as hare-brained business schemes that feed management's ego but are not sound business propositions. Managers may not police the activities of their employees; they may be reluctant to fire people who are no longer useful to the company; or they may give in to excessive wage demands. It has also been argued that managers, left on their own, will try to make the company as big as possible, even if doing so is economically inefficient and reduces the likelihood of future profits.[24] One way of making the company big is to refuse to pay out the earnings as dividends, and instead to reinvest them in the company.

All of these are potential problems when management is not subject to the restriction of making profits and distributing them to the shareholders. Of course, managers might also use this freedom for good purposes. They might show a more sympathetic attitude toward resolving their labor problems; they might give to local charities; they might show more integrity than the law requires. Whether they behave thus depends on the "corporate culture" that reigns; at some times and places, management may behave in an enlightened manner when set free. But there is no reason to expect that the net impact of turning the entrenched management loose (with no restrictions) to make profits will generally cause them to use their freedom in a selfless, enlightened, manner.

With the renewed concentration of investment holdings among institutional investors, the control could, in principle, pass not to the ultimate owners, but to professional representatives of the owners. The rise of institutional investors may thus herald an end to the problems that Berle and Means described. There may now be reason to think that institutional investors have more things on their minds than the purely speculative considerations that some have argued dominates their thinking.

Even if this is the trend, at present, institutional investors do not seem to be using their power to influence the corporations in which they hold shares. The average institutional investor sells 40 percent of its stock holdings within a year's time from purchase.[25] When investors hold shares for so short a time, then they cannot get to know a company's operations well, and cannot participate effectively in the management of the company.

There is some evidence that institutional investors are beginning to play a more active role in the management of the firms in which they own shares. This trend was noted as early as the beginning of the 1980s.[26] Many institutional investors testify that this group is now more active, and there are a number of examples of institutional investor activism in recent years.[27] For example, in 1987, the California Public Employees' Retirement System and the New York State Employees' Retirement Fund asked the CEO of Texaco for a role in nominating directors to the Texaco board; by 1989, Texaco accepted a nomination from them. In 1989, the California Public Employees' Retirement System and the Pennsylvania Public School Employees' Retirement System initiated and won a proxy fight against two anti-takeover measures backed by the management of Honeywell, Inc. In 1989, the Detroit Policemen and Firemen Retirement System together with the Detroit General Retirement System initiated a hostile takeover to replace management of Income Opportunity Trust, a company in which these institutions held stock. According to a recent *Fortune* article, in 1990, institutions put forward a record ninety-eight shareholder resolutions in proxy contests, of which thirteen won a plurality of votes.[28]

These trends in institutional intervention in the management of the companies in which they own stock may herald the beginning of active participation in management by institutional investors, and the beginning of the end of the loss of ownership control that Berle and Means documented. Institutions, however, appear to have a long way to go before such activism is the norm, and, as a group, they will have to adopt a policy of lower portfolio turnover before they can be serious about such activism.

Various laws and regulations in the United States may inhibit shareholder participation.[29] While the Securities Act of 1934 was supposed to encourage shareholder participation by making rules that facilitate proxy voting, in fact, some of the rules work to inhibit it. The shareholder proposal rule (Rule 14a-8) bars access on three kinds of shareholder proposals: director nominations, statements in opposition to management proposals, and alternatives to management proposals. The Exchange Act Section 13(d) put groups of shareholders who act together in a voting initiative at risk of lawsuits from the management of the company; such a threat serves to discourage such initiatives, whether or not management actually sues. Court decisions permitting poison pills may also serve to discourage organizing a shareholder group for any voting purpose.[30]

Laws in other countries encourage greater shareholder participation in management of the companies in which they hold stock and, as a result, in some other countries there is much more institutional input into management decisions. For example, most major Japanese firms maintain close relations with a particular bank, known as the firm's main bank, and close relations with a grouping of firms, known as a keiretsu.[31] The main bank for a given firm does not have any legal status as such, but there exists a general recognition among capital market participants that firms are tied to a main bank. The managements of the main bank and of the other companies in the keiretsu generally have substantial, though minority, stakes in each of the firms in the keiretsu. Moreover, they tend to be permanent stockholders, unlike American institutional investors, which are in and out of a firm often in less than a year.

Interaction with the keiretsu or the main bank is thought to contribute good discipline and support for managers, providing a sort of "structured dissent" over the activities of the firm—the kind of dissent that Louis Lowenstein and others hope that institutional investors in the United States will provide in the future.[32]

## 78 ◆ WHO'S MINDING THE STORE?

As an example of the impact of this structured dissent on a Japanese company, consider the case of Toyo Kogyo, a member of the Sumitomo keiretsu.[33] In 1974, Kohei Matsuda, the president of the firm and grandson of the founder, insisted on continuing and expanding production of their Mazda car with a rotary engine, despite great evidence that demand for the fuel-hungry car would decline with higher oil prices. Toyo Kogyo dealers from around Japan complained to Sumitomo Bank officials. Later that year, Sumitomo sent two of its senior officers to join Toyo Kogyo's management; over the next two years Sumitomo Bank and Sumitomo Trust placed eleven of their executives in the management of Toyo Kogyo, and Kohei Matsuda was relieved of operating duties. It would be extremely unlikely for American institutional investors to intervene in the management of a company in such a way—even if a small group of these investors owned the majority of shares; they might do no more to express their dissatisfaction than sell the shares.

There is supposed to be a sort of structured dissent among American corporations—analogous to that in Japan—in the form of outside directors. Because these directors are chosen from outside the company, they are not caught up in the culture of that company and are not dependent on the management of that company for their own career advancement. In practice, however, these outside directors cannot substitute for the management of another company with a major financial interest in the success of the company.

Samuel B. Graves and Sandra A. Waddock speculate that if institutional investors in the United States begin to play a more active role in management, they will function as the "conglomerate of the 1990s."[34] The conglomerate movement of the 1960s in the United States saw the emergence of conglomerates with a central management presiding over a number of divisions in unrelated businesses. The managements of the conglomerates become, in effect, institutional investors who own all—rather than just a small fraction—of the stock in the firms in which they invest, and they do not expect to turn over their holdings in their divisions. They have an advantage over institutional investors in that they have complete access to information about the activities of their "investments." These conglomerates would seem to be analogous to the keiretsu, with the management of the conglomerate analogous to the main bank.

When conglomerates were first formed they were believed to offer certain efficiency advantages.[35] But conglomerates are often viewed today as unsuccessful, and the 1980s saw a trend toward the breakup of conglomerates. One theory why conglomerates have not performed better is that central managements of conglomerates were too distant from, and

## Disruptions Caused by Hostile Takeovers

ignorant of, the businesses in their various divisions.[36] Consequently, they were forced to judge division managers by short-term financial measures and failed to encourage strategic or long-term thinking. There is a risk that the same problem could arise in a system with activist institutional investors.

A tender offer is an offer to buy all—or part—of the shares that shareholders of a target company decide to offer or tender; it is hostile if it is undertaken without prior approval of the management of the target company. Until around 1960, hostile tender offers hardly had been used to take over companies in the United States. But starting in the early 1960s, and extending through the 1980s, these hostile tender offers began to be seen for "underpriced" stocks. (Underpriced stocks are stocks that seem to have more value to someone who could gain control of a company than the price per share would imply.) In the course of the hostile takeover, the price that the target company's stocks commanded would usually jump dramatically.

The cause of the increase in price—often 80 percent or more—occasioned by these hostile tender offers has been the subject of some debate. According to conventional Wall Street wisdom, the price increase need mean nothing more than that one must pay a premium to buy large quantities of shares or to provide motivation for investors to sell stocks they have not been considering selling (to provoke them out of their inertia). Following this theory, the price increases are related to investor behavior that would be classified as speculative: the stock was underpriced by investors before, or overpriced afterward, or both. An alternative theory, favored by those who believe in the efficient-markets hypothesis, discussed above, has also often been offered. According to this theory, the price increase represents a genuine increase in value of the target company—because after the takeover, the business would be run differently or the assets that the management of the target company was sitting on would be paid out as dividends.

The takeover movement gained some impetus from the development of "junk" bonds, which also flourished in the 1980s. The money to make tender offers was raised by issuing high-risk (junk) bonds to the public. These junk bonds are inherently high risk in many takeover situations because the principal can be repaid only from the payout of the investment in the target firm at a price far above the original market price of the firm. The development of junk bonds is not any great invention; rather, the proliferation of these bonds represents the success of a sales

## 80 ◆ Who's Minding the Store?

promotion, which convinced many investors that these bonds were safe.

Those who promoted tender offers for takeovers claimed that their junk bonds were relatively safe, since the new management after the takeover would create value represented by the takeover-induced high share prices. Others countered with skepticism, claiming that the high premiums paid for shares of the target firm in tender offers were, in effect, speculative excesses, caused by false optimism. They argued that the past default record on low-quality bonds, cited by the promoters of those bonds, was no indication that there would not be many defaults on these new junk bonds. The collapse of the junk bond market in 1990 suggests that, whatever the merits of the skeptics' argument, the value that was supposedly created by many of the takeovers was not there.

Whether the takeover-related price changes are a good thing depends on whether these takeover-induced share price increases reflect true efficiency gains or speculative price increases. Financial economist Michael Jensen has argued that the price increases come about because the new system of management in the post-takeover firm sometimes encourages much more efficiency and the pay out of free cash flow (defined as the excess of that required to fund all profitable investment projects).[37] The more efficient management comes about, in theory, because the new organizations provide better incentives to management: Management is typically given a major share in the profits of a corporation after a takeover, and the corporation is so highly leveraged that risk of bankruptcy puts the managers' "backs to the wall" in search of ways to improve cash flow. This pressure to pay off the debt also forces managers to distribute free cash flow. If this is what happens, we might think that the takeover-induced price increase was justified by the increased distributors to shareholders that the takeover caused.

Some studies assert that they found evidence supporting the claim that the performance of firms that have been taken over does improve after better incentives to management are in place. Two such studies—one by Frank R. Lichtenberg and Donald Siegel, and one by Steven Kaplan—looked at firms taken private in management buyouts and concluded that both financial and real performance measures improved after the buyouts.[38] These studies were criticized, though, by Scott B. Smart and Joel Waldfogel, on the grounds that firms that are taken private may tend to be ones that the management already knows have the prospect of improved performance; indeed, they argue, management has an incentive to take a firm private at a time when its outlook temporarily looks, to outsiders, worse than it is.[39]

The other view of these takeovers is that the attendant price increases—the takeover premiums—are unwarranted speculative price increases, caused by the same psychological forces in the markets that create other speculative excesses. If this is true, then some takeovers created a lot of unnecessary disruption for certain individuals: employees whose jobs were terminated, communities whose local economies suffered, and suppliers of the company whose own businesses suffered. This disruption may then extend to the company's operations, should the company's employees, as a result of the disruption become cynical and unmotivated.

The takeover movement of the 1980s appears now to be largely over. With the collapse of the junk-bond market, it has become much harder to raise funds for takeovers. Moreover, so much opposition was generated to the takeovers of the 1980s that many state laws were passed and court decisions rendered that make takeovers more difficult: Since the 1982 *Edgar v. MITE Corp.* Supreme Court decision, which upheld an Illinois anti-takeover law, at least twenty-nine states have passed new anti-takeover laws. At least four hundred corporations have adopted poison pills to prevent takeovers, and the courts have allowed these to stand. The courts have also generally allowed the business judgment rule (that a court will not interfere with the running of a corporation by its officers and directors just for their mistake in judgment, so long as their action was in good faith) to apply to defensive actions against takeovers when independent directors approve. Approximately twenty-five states have adopted multi-constituency laws that redefine a directors' fiduciary duty as owed not just to shareholders but also to many other constituencies as well.[40]

The strongest of the multi-constituency laws is also the most recent, and it may signal a new trend. The Pennsylvania anti-takeover law, which took effect in April 1990, allows management to give first consideration to employees, customers, suppliers, or the community—rather than to shareholders—in weighing takeover bids. Such laws as the Pennsylvania anti-takeover law enable a board of directors to say no to a generous cash offer for the company. They might wish to do so for selfish reasons, such as to preserve their jobs, under the guise of concern for others. Moreover, proxy fights for control of a corporation are discouraged by a "disgorgement" provision in the Pennsylvania law, which raises the potential costs to mounting a takeover attempt: The provision states that any person or institution owning more than 20 percent of a company's shares must forfeit any profit on those shares if they are sold within eighteen months after a failed buyout or proxy fight.

Critics of the Pennsylvania and other multi-constituency laws argue that the general discretion these laws give to directors in weighing the importance of the interests of various stakeholders makes ambiguous the purpose of the corporation and increases the possibility that directors will abuse their trust. There is, indeed, a risk that such multi-constituency

## 82 ◆ Who's Minding the Store?

laws will reduce the productivity of corporations. Dealing more specifically with the grievances of the various stakeholders in corporations may require more specific legislation in the 1990s.

### Derivative Markets and Short-Term Speculation

Great concern has been expressed about the growing volume of trade in the stock index futures markets ever since their institution in 1982 and about the degree to which the speculators on these markets were making the stock market more volatile. *Barron's* ran a long article on December 10, 1984, headlined "Is the Tail Wagging the Dog? Sizing Up the Impact of Stock Index Futures on the Market." *The Wall Street Journal* and other influential publications raised similar concerns, and these concerns continue to be echoed today.

There is no a priori reason to expect the advent of stock index futures markets to increase volatility. These futures markets make it cheaper to trade, but there is no presumption that cheaper trading brings into the market either more destabilizing or more stabilizing traders. Destabilizing speculation occurs when those who are trading think that price increases portend further price increases, and price decreases further price decreases. There is no way of knowing whether the people who hold this opinion are among the more sensitive to costs of trading securities.

The stock index futures markets are, in effect, just other stock markets where baskets of stocks represented by the indexes are traded. In fact, no shares are actually traded; rather, in effect, bets are made on the future course of the stock price indexes.[41] Still, the index futures markets are, in effect, just other stock markets, because these markets are linked by arbitrageurs to the actual stock markets. Essentially the same is true of the index options markets and of the growing variety of over-the-counter equity derivatives or "synthetic equities" offered by dealers.[42]

Those who do the trading that links the different markets are doing what is called index arbitrage: the simultaneous or near simultaneous buying or selling of stock and selling or buying of index futures to profit with little risk from the price difference between the futures market and the stock market. If the futures price is above the cash price (plus a certain margin representing the arbitrageur's costs) of the stocks represented by the index, the index arbitrageur sells the futures and buys the portfolio of stocks represented by the index, thereby locking in a sure profit. If the futures price is below the cash price by a certain margin, the arbitrageur buys the futures and shorts the portfolio of stocks.

Competition among index arbitrageurs reduces both the price discrepancies and the profits to be made in index arbitrage. Movements in prices in the stock markets will be communicated via index arbitrageurs to the futures markets, and conversely; that is as it should be if there is to be only one price for the basket of stocks represented by the index.

To make index arbitrage worthwhile requires buying or selling large amounts of baskets of stocks; this is because competition among index arbitrageurs insures that the price discrepancies among the cash, futures, and other equity-derivatives markets are normally very small. According to a recent New York Stock Exchange study: "Calculations suggest that index arbitrage has become so competitive that the return from textbook-style riskless index arbitrage can rarely match Treasury bill rates. . . . Because riskless arbitrage is rarely profitable, most transactions currently labeled as index arbitrage are likely to be speculative quasi-arbitrage strategies whereby the arbitrageur accepts some risk in the hope of earning a higher return."[43]

Kenneth A. Froot, James F. Gammil, Jr., and Andre F. Perold have investigated whether the predictability of stock market returns has changed substantially since 1983.[44] Destabilizing speculation might be evidenced by a predictability of returns, say a tendency for inertia in prices. They found that, in 1983, there was substantial positive serial correlation of fifteen-minute S&P 500 returns with lagged fifteen-minute returns; a tendency for price increases to be followed by later price increases; decreases, by later decreases. By 1989, that positive inertia had almost vanished. They hypothesize that the advent of futures markets and the decline in dealers' commissions have made markets more efficient rather than less.

If we may extrapolate to financial futures markets from other futures markets, we can probably safely say that the establishment of these markets does not tend to increase market volatility or excessive speculation. One survey of the literature on the effects of the establishment of futures markets concluded that almost all studies found no subsequent increase in market volatility.[45]

## DECLINES IN COST OF TRADING AND STOCK MARKET VOLATILITY

Part of the increase in turnover in stocks in recent decades is due to the decline in transaction costs brought about by deregulation. This has raised concerns that the lower transaction costs encourage excessive speculation. In the United States, brokerage fees were made competitive by a 1975 act of Congress. In the United Kingdom, the "Big Bang" deregulation in 1986 cut brokerage charges there, and other European countries have followed suit. With lower brokerage charges, the volume of trade should increase. But these declines in brokerage costs are not likely to explain all of the increase in turnover—turnover that has occurred gradually since 1978, rather than on a one-shot basis on the dates of deregulation.

There is a positive correlation, historically, between volume of trade and volatility of prices of stocks.[46] Thus, it is natural to consider whether the increased stock price volatility observed in connection with the stock market crash of 1987 might be related to the high volume of trade and, hence, to either the lowering of brokerage commissions that induced higher turnover or the institution of futures and other derivative markets.

But, since 1982, the changes in volatility (as measured by the standard deviation of percentage price index changes) do not match up well with the increase in volume on the stock index futures markets. The year 1987 was an isolated year of high volatility, surrounded by years of more nearly normal price volatility.[47] Perhaps the impression of high volatility occurs because the Dow Jones Industrial Average is at record high levels, so that the number of points the index moves on a given day tends to be unusually large by historical standards. The high level of the Dow Jones Industrial Average is partly just due to price inflation, which makes all prices higher. The proper measure of volatility is a measure of the dispersion of the percentage change.

Research does not point to any other likely explanations for the changes in stock market volatility observed through time. The changing volatility of the market appears to have a life of its own, unrelated to financial innovations such as the institution of futures markets or the decline of transactions costs associated with deregulation. Perhaps we should not be surprised that there isn't more of an association of volatility with these events; to the extent that volatility is induced by speculative behavior, and is associated with changing popular interest and popular theories about the stock market, there is no reason to expect that we should be able to explain volatility in simple terms.

Chapter Five

# Measures for Dealing with Speculation and Short-Termism

The problems caused by excessive speculation are difficult to deal with without creating major new problems. Thus, not surprisingly, the major policy measures that have been proposed may not seem like exciting new initiatives; they are just modest changes in tax rates or in regulations. This is not to say, however, that adoption of such measures is not an important priority, given the significance of the problems with which they deal.

In this chapter I will discuss some of the major proposed policy measures—those that have received the most public discussion recently. These are transactions taxes, capital gains taxes with holding-period restrictions, increased margin requirements, circuit breakers, and measures to encourage shareholder participation in corporate governance.

## TRANSACTIONS TAXES

Imposition of taxes on the purchase and sale of securities has been among the proposals discussed recently for the purpose of reducing speculative activity in stocks.[1] The idea of using transactions taxes for this purpose is much older. In 1936, Keynes wrote: "The introduction of a substantial government transfer tax on all transactions might prove to be the most serviceable reform available, with a view to mitigating the predominance of speculation over enterprise in the United States."[2]

Taxes on the purchase or sale of securities have a long history. In the United Kingdom, stamp duties on the transfer of securities were introduced during the reign of Queen Anne in 1714. The stamp duties on sales of U.S. stocks appeared in laws and resolutions relating to the direct and excise taxes enacted by the 37th Congress in 1863. But the tax rate was quite low. From 1898 to 1931, the rate was 0.02 percent; from 1932 to 1944, it was 0.05 percent; from 1945 to 1955, 0.06 percent; and from 1956 to 1965, it was 0.04 percent. The stamp tax on transfers of corporate stocks was abolished in 1965.

These stamp taxes appear to have been imposed for the sake of revenue collection. The tax rate was set in consideration of fairness in comparison with other excise taxes, and in consideration of the impact of these taxes on the income of stockbrokers as compared with producers of other goods subject to excise taxes. Because the excise taxes were set to extract only a "fair" fraction of brokers' incomes, the tax rates were set at a fraction of typical retail brokerage charges and did not represent a substantial disincentive to retail trade in stocks. The elimination of the stamp taxes on the transfer of securities in 1965 was part of a general reduction of excise taxes, which were then eliminated (except on such undesirables as alcohol and tobacco and on goods and services for which the excise tax may be considered a user charge).

In contrast with the U.S. experience, other countries still have substantial transactions taxes on transfers of corporate shares. However, with the globalization of markets, it may no longer be possible to allow the present kind of discrepancies in tax rates across countries. For example, Sweden has a high transfer tax, and it has been claimed that as a result many Swedish stocks are traded primarily not in Sweden but in London.[3] Imposition of high tax rates on the transfer of securities cannot be achieved without special arrangements to prevent nationals from taking their transactions abroad.

Transactions taxes are supposed to help reduce excessive speculation by discouraging people from buying or selling. The idea is that buying or selling will become such a rare event that when one does buy or sell, one assumes that the decision will be final for many years. In that case, one would be inclined, the theory goes, to take less into account the probable behavior of market prices in the ensuing months, and look instead at the value of the stream of anticipated dividends in the near future.

But things may not be so simple. Someone who is about to buy or sell still has reason to consider whether to postpone buying or selling to a short while hence, when prices may become more favorable. Prices are still set by the outcome of supply and demand of those who *do* buy and sell, and these people may have just as much of an incentive to time the purchases of their buying and selling as if there were no transactions tax. Moreover, consider a time when a speculative boom is under way. Indeed, transactions taxes might have the useful effect of discouraging some traders from buying into the boom—an effect that prevents them from providing it more fuel. But transactions taxes would also have the harmful effect of discouraging others (who think that the boom has gone on too long) from selling into the boom—an effect that prevents them from acting to stabilize the market.

Of course, transactions taxes impose burdens by making it expensive to engage in trades—nonspeculative as well as speculative. The cost might be mitigated by varying the transaction tax in response to indicators of speculative activity. The transactions tax could kick in only on high-volume days; or the exchanges themselves could engage in peak-load pricing, raising commission rates on high-volume days. The effects of such conditional transactions taxes could be many and varied, depending on the rules used to impose them. If transactions taxes depended on volume of trade, for example, certain kinds of investors would be given an incentive to wait out a stock market crash until another day when transactions taxes are lower; it cannot be predicted a priori what effect the absence of these particular investors on the day of a crash would imply for market prices on these days, since we do not know what kinds of theories or ideas these people have.

Transactions taxes might have some benefit in reducing excessive speculative activity, but they achieve this at the cost of discouraging trade—making it harder for people to get into or out of their investments. Because of the latter costs, proposers of transactions taxes keep the proposed rate small—less than 2 percent, perhaps—not enough to offset the decline in transactions costs caused by deregulation of brokers' commissions in 1975. Ultimately, then, the transactions taxes will have less effect on excessive speculation than do capital gains taxes, which have been much higher.

## HOLDING-PERIOD RESTRICTIONS AND CAPITAL GAINS TAXES

Capital gains taxes that are imposed selectively on capital gains received over short holding periods also have been advocated as a means of controlling speculative excesses.[4] They provide a tax disincentive for quick profit taking, thereby weakening the attractiveness of some speculative strategies.

The United States imposes no capital gains taxes on institutional investors (such as pension funds) because these institutions are themselves untaxed. On the assumption that a capital gains tax for gains over short holding periods on pension funds would discourage churning and speculation, Senator Nancy Kassebaum introduced a bill entitled the Excessive Churning and Speculation Act of 1989. This bill would impose on pension funds a 10 percent tax on capital gains from assets held 30 days or less, and a 5 percent tax on capital gains from assets held for longer than 30 but not longer than 180 days. The holding-period requirements are supposed to discourage short-term trading and leave untaxed any pension funds that do not trade quickly.

The Kassebaum bill is not without precedent. When preferential treatment of capital gains was first instituted in 1921, concern with speculation was given as the reason for requiring a two-year holding period; since then, the discouragement of speculation was repeatedly offered in debates as a reason for such holding-period requirements until the repeal of preferential treatment in 1986.[5] What is new in the Kassebaum bill is the imposition of capital gains tax with a holding-period requirement on previously untaxed entities—the pension funds. Even this is not entirely without precedent. The Internal Revenue Code already contains an analogous holding-period requirement for institutional investors, aimed at discouraging speculation. This is called the short-short rule: Regulated investment companies (or mutual funds) must derive less than 30 percent of their gross income from sale or exchange of securities held for less than three months if they are to retain their status as flow-through entities for tax purposes. Otherwise, the income of the mutual fund will be taxed.

Capital gains taxes with holding-period requirements are supposed to discourage speculative trading and thereby reduce speculative behavior. It is indeed possible that capital gains taxes will have such an effect. It was noted above that survey evidence shows much speculative behavior appears to be undertaken with the expectation that the investment will be unwound in six to twelve months. If people speculate with this expectation, then their prospective up-side potential will be diminished by a capital gains tax on short-term profits. The number of such people who are active in speculation will tend to be diminished.

But this is hardly the only logical consequence of such taxes. Other effects of capital gains taxes on short-term capital gains may serve to increase the effects of speculative price changes. Suppose a speculative bubble should start, in which prices begin to rise because investors worry about price rises. A capital gains tax like that proposed by Kassebaum need not discourage investors from attempting to buy stocks, and so the tax would not have the immediate impact of restricting the speculative price increase. It might also have the effect of discouraging some pension fund managers (who had purchased recently and who did not share in the speculative fervor) from selling. The effect of the capital gains taxes might then be to restrict the supply of stocks, and therefore to exacerbate, not mitigate, the boom. Suppose also that the boom ends in a stock market crash. Some investors will then have an incentive to sell to obtain a capital loss for tax purposes (offsetting other short-term gains they have previously realized), possibly exacerbating the crash.[6]

There is other evidence suggesting perhaps a weak effect on excessive speculation of holding-period requirements that tax shorter-term capital gains at a higher rate. Homeowners in the United States are allowed, after age fifty-five, a one-time-only opportunity to sell their home without paying a capital gains tax. Those who are younger than fifty-five who sell a house must buy another house of equal or higher value within eighteen months to avoid having to pay a capital gains tax. This provision has not prevented speculative booms. Some striking booms of housing prices were seen in various cities in the United States in the 1980s, and there is evidence that some of these were speculative booms and not caused primarily by changes in such things as population or average incomes.[7] The effect of these holding-period restrictions may have been to reduce the probability of speculative crashes, since, once people buy a house, they feel locked in by the capital gains until they retire. People speak of moving from a high-price to a low-price area, and feeling constrained to buy a much bigger house than they desire just to avoid paying capital gains taxes. The result, despite the absence of sudden major crashes, is a major misallocation of housing resources; some people sit in enormous houses that they do not want, and others who want houses are continuously priced out of the housing market.

In any event, capital gains taxes should be indexed to inflation so that the tax is on real, not just nominal, capital gains. Unindexed capital gains taxes impose essentially a random element to the taxation, penalizing asset holders for the national inflation rate.

## MARGIN REQUIREMENTS

Margin requirements on holdings of speculative assets were first mandated by the Securities Exchange Act of 1934, in reaction to the stock market crash of 1929. Margin credit had been widely reported and followed prior to the stock market crash, and excessive margin credit was widely seen then as a major cause of the boom before the crash. Margin calls were seen as a factor promoting the crash; initial price declines forced selling in response to margin calls, which produced further price declines.

## 90 ◆ WHO'S MINDING THE STORE?

In contrast to transactions costs, which serve to discourage trading of stocks, margin requirements discourage some investors from holding stocks. The effect of margin requirements differs across investors, depending on their portfolios and desired quantities of stocks held. If the investors who are feeding a speculative boom are compulsive gamblers who are wheedling their relatives to borrow money to put into the stock market, then margin requirements are likely to be effective. But those feeding a speculative boom might just as well be people who have no such borrowing needs; they may be ordinary people who just theorize that the market will go up.

The effectiveness of margin requirements has been substantially mitigated by the advent of the futures markets in derivative instruments, which have not been made subject to the regulation imposed on equity markets. If margin requirements reduce volatility, then the advent of stock index futures markets would plausibly herald an increase in stock market volatility. That apparently has not happened yet, though the evidence since 1982 is not enough to be conclusive, since other factors influence volatility through time.

The original impetus for margin requirements was apparently to prevent irresponsible or emotional investors from borrowing heavily to buy into a speculative boom; thus margin requirements could help prevent a speculative boom. But since margin requirements might also limit the ability of investors from buying into a crash situation, and provide no disincentives for selling, they may worsen the effect of a crash.

Indeed, individual investors were net buyers on the stock index futures markets on both October 19 and 20, 1987, and so margin requirements (which primarily affect individual investors) apparently worsened the crash. The largest sellers on these days were pension funds, trusts, and other institutional portfolio managers.[8]

There does seem to be some evidence suggesting that margin requirements can have a stabilizing effect on stock markets. Economists Gikas Hardouvelis and Steve Peristiani produced charts showing the average change in stock prices before and after increases or decreases in margin requirements in both the United States and Japan.[9] In both countries, margin requirements tend to be increased after a period of rising stock prices, and the trend of rising stock prices is immediately reversed on the date of the margin requirement change. In Japan (and less clearly in the United States), margin requirements tend to be decreased after a period of declining stock prices, and the downward trend is, on average, immediately replaced by an upward trend. These effects might, however, occur because the margin requirement change is a signal of other policy changes as well.[10]

## CIRCUIT BREAKERS

One of the prime recommendations of the Brady Commission (the Presidential Task Force on Market Mechanisms) following the 1987 stock market crash was the institution of "circuit breakers" that would shut down the stock market as well as derivative markets in the event of another stock market crash; these circuit breakers would be coordinated across the exchanges.[11] In response to the commission's recommendations, on July 7, 1988, the New York Stock Exchange together with the Chicago Mercantile Exchange announced some coordinated circuit breakers. These new rules specify that all stock trading on the New York Stock Exchange will be halted for one hour if the Dow Jones Industrial Average falls 250 points during one day, and for an additional two hours if the average falls another 150 points (for a total of 400 points) on the same day. The rules now also specify that, when the primary S&P 500 futures contract on the Chicago Mercantile Exchange declines 12 points (or approximately 100 points on the Dow Jones Industrial Average), no trades below that level are allowed for another 30 minutes; when the contract declines another 8 points on the same day (so that the total decline is 20 points), no trades below that level are allowed for one hour.

Circuit breakers are supposed to prevent a panic from turning into a free fall, by allowing time for buyers to come into the market. Some market participants seem to like a rule that gives them some time to think and collect information at a time of sudden market moves. (It also gives them time to keep up with regulatory requirements—such as margin requirements.) However, the ultimate impact of the circuit breakers, by suspending trading only for a matter of minutes, depends (in ways that cannot be foretold on theoretical grounds) on how people behave when a circuit breaker is about to be imposed, and on how they behave after the markets are opened again.

The knowledge among traders that a circuit breaker exists might cause them to try to get out of the market before the circuit breaker is imposed. This "gravitational effect" may cause the price to fall and cause the circuit breaker to be imposed.[12] After the markets open again, it may turn out that investors have reached even more negative opinions about the outlook for the market while waiting for the markets to reopen. In contrast, it may be recalled that according to some accounts of the day after the stock market crash, October 20, 1987, investor confidence made a critical upturn when a futures contract, the Major Market Index (the remaining major contract that had not been closed), suddenly rallied.[13]

Although the circuit breakers have not yet had the effect of closing the major stock exchanges, it may be helpful to look at the examples of market closings we have always had—the weekend closings of the markets. Wednesday, Thursday, and Friday, October 14 through 16, 1987, saw dramatic stock price drops. People had plenty of time to think over the following weekend, but there was no recovery from the panic, and Monday, October 19, was the worst one-day stock market crash in history. On the other hand, the stock market drop of Friday, October 13, 1989, which caused the news media on that Friday to raise the alarming possibility of another Monday crash, was followed by generally reassuring commentary by market analysts and economists over the weekend. There was no crash the following Monday. Clearly, the predictable effect of a circuit breaker is just that it gives people more time to think before they take their next action; what they actually do then depends on the conclusions they reach.[14]

## MEASURES TO ENCOURAGE SHAREHOLDER PARTICIPATION IN CORPORATE GOVERNANCE

There has been a lot of discussion of how to solve the problems created by the separation of ownership and control and by the tendency of investors to sell their shares when dissatisfied with the management of a firm, rather than to make efforts to correct problems in the firm. Proposed solutions include changing regulations that restrict proxy votes to encourage shareholder proposals, and instituting "structured dissent" within corporations (to bring our system closer to the Japanese system, where management is less independent).

The Securities and Exchange Commission has recently proposed changed proxy rules to encourage shareholder communications. They proposed Rule 14A-X, which would allow substantial shareholders who have held stock in a company for a prescribed period of time to have mailed with the company's proxy statement a short statement with their opinion about the quality of the management.

Advocates of greater investor input into corporate decisionmaking, Louis Lowenstein and Michael T. Jacobs recommend dealing with entrenched managements by instituting a system that would force genuine representatives of shareholders onto the boards of directors of the nation's corporations.[15] According to their concept, a substantial fraction of boards of directors would be shareholder nominated. Their remedy also would provide the opportunity and incentive for outside management teams to dissent from the strategies of the company's managers.

Ronald Gilson and Reinier Kraakman have proposed creating a class of full-time professional outside directors, each of whom would sit on a number of boards as representatives of institutional investors.[16] These directors, who would be economically dependent on institutional investors, would receive substantial compensation—sufficient to encourage talented people to take such a job—and they would have no other major time commitments.

John C. Coffee of the Columbia Law School has proposed relaxing the standards for diversification for institutional investors, so that institutional investors can hold fewer financial assets in their portfolios.[17] He points out that, with the growth of indexation of portfolios, many institutional investors are holding virtually all 500 stocks in the Standard and Poor Composite Index—so many stocks that they have little substantial interest in any one. These institutional investors have little incentive to participate in governance of any of the companies in which they hold shares. Diversification that is fairly effective in reducing portfolio risk could be achieved with far fewer stocks.

Proposals to improve shareholder participation have received substantial attention in the United Kingdom, too. Nicholas Ridley, the United Kingdom's trade and industry secretary, has proposed encouraging shareholders' committees among institutional investors, a strengthened role for nonexecutive directors, and a right for major shareholders to appoint a majority of board members.[18]

There has been some dispute over how much can be done to encourage more institutional participation in managerial decisions without destroying the liquidity that institutional investors enjoy. The general trend around the world is for increasing reliance on world markets, away from the regional relationships that characterized much investment activities in the past. Gilson and Kraakman as well as Bernard Black have argued that, despite this trend, changed regulations and institutions could induce much more shareholder participation in management of firms; Coffee does not believe that most changes will be very effective.[19]

Chapter Six

# Discount Rates and Saving Rates

In the discussion in previous chapters, the term "short-termism" has referred to a tendency among both investors and corporate managers to be excessively concerned with the market response—in terms of price per share—rather than with the long-run outlook for earnings of a corporation. This kind of short-termism arises because many people pay attention to the market rather than to fundamentals, and because these people do not believe that the market tracks fundamentals. There is, however, another kind of short-termism that is conceptually distinct from the above, though in some ways related to it. This latter kind of short-termism is a fundamental lack, among the general public, of regard for long-run planning. This latter kind of short-termism may be measured in two ways: as too high a discount rate (that is, cost of capital) applied to investments, and too little savings.

The discount rate or cost of capital is the real interest rate that the market uses to discount future real income into today's price. We are all familiar with one kind of discount rate—the interest rate on a savings bond or a treasury bill. When one buys one of these financial instruments, one pays less than the face value of the instrument; this principal is payable only on the maturity date some time in the future. (These instruments do not pay regular interest; all one receives is the fixed principal at the maturity date.) One buys the instrument at a discount from its face value, and the deeper the discount, the higher the return one gets from the investment; in general, the rate of return implicit in the discount in any such investment is called the discount rate.

We can, by analogy, think of the price of a share in a corporation at any time as the present discounted value of all the future dividends paid to the owner of the share. Indeed, owning a share is like owning a portfolio of savings bonds, whose maturities correspond to future dividend payments, starting from the time of the next dividend payment, out to the indefinite future; and the price of a share may be thought of as the sum of the present discounted values of all these future dividends. Of course, these future dividends are not guaranteed by the government; they are uncertain today. But those who participate in the stock market have some expectation of the likely amounts of these payments, and the price today reflects both these expectations and the rate at which they are discounted to today's price per share. Short-termism, if defined as too high a discount rate, then means, not that prices in the stock market are too speculative or too volatile, but that they are too low—that is, that people do not value these long-term investments enough.[1] It means that people are too impatient for things today, and do not care enough about future income.

The saving rate is a more familiar concept: it is the proportion of income that people save, set aside to help earn future income. The amount that people save (and put in the bank or invest in financial assets) determines the amount of resources that are available for real investments: for building plant and equipment, for improving land, for building apartments and houses, for things that will yield income in the future. Short-termism, if defined as too low a saving rate, then means that not enough resources are being made available for such real investments.

Too high a discount rate tends to go hand in hand with too low a saving rate; both may be caused by a tendency to disregard the future. If people care little about the future, they may both save too little and place too low a value on assets that pay dividends in the future. By saving too little, they create a shortage of funds for real investments, and so the only real investments that are made are those that have a high return. For example, a factory might not be built that would yield substantial income in the future, since the rate of return on the investment in the factory is just not high enough to satisfy the investors in the market; the potential future income from the factory is just not enticing enough to make people willing to invest in the factory today. Many of us are not accustomed to thinking that too low a saving rate goes hand in hand with too low a level of prices in the stock market. But, in fact, if we persuaded people to want to save more, the immediate impact would likely be an upward surge in stock prices. By trying to save more, people would bid up the prices of stocks.

## Concerns that the Discount Rate Is Too High

Over sixty years ago, the prominent economist A. C. Pigou made the influential argument that human society tends to place too high a discount rate on everything, due to an irrational impatience, a foolish desire for pleasure now relative to the future. While his argument was made long ago, he claimed that he was addressing a basic principle of human nature, and so we can expect that the same argument applies today.

Now, economists have long been very reluctant to call people irrational, and prefer instead to say on this matter that people merely have a preference or taste for present pleasures over future ones. Pigou countered their arguments:

> But this preference for present pleasures does not—the idea is self-contradictory—imply that a present pleasure of given magnitude is any *greater* than a future pleasure of the same magnitude. It implies only that our telescopic faculty is defective, and that we, therefore, see future pleasures, as it were, on a diminished scale. That this is the right explanation is proved by the fact that exactly the same diminution is experienced when, apart from our tendency to forget ungratifying incidents, we contemplate the past. Hence the existence of preference for present over equally certain future pleasures does not imply that any economic dissatisfaction would be suffered if future pleasures were substituted at full value for present ones.[2]

Given this "irrational" behavior, people would benefit from government policies that encouraged them to use a lower rate of discount; the effect would be to cause them to place more value on any given earnings flow.

Moreover, Pigou stressed that the market rate of discount is too low in a different sense: the rate is influenced only by the people who are alive today and does not reflect the preferences of the yet-to-be-born. He thought that the duty of government policymakers is to "protect the interests of the future *in some degree* against the effects of our irrational discounting and of our preference for ourselves over our descendants."[3] This irrational discounting causes there to be too little real investment for the future, and thus too little investment made for future generations. He urged intervention in the market to encourage savings and investment through a system of bounties and taxes.

Research shows that errors people make extend beyond the *level* of discount rates used.[4] People do not apply consistent discount rates to investment decisions. For example, the economist Jerry Hausman showed that individuals purchasing air conditioners, and having to decide between models of varying energy efficiency (a decision involving a tradeoff between purchase price and delayed energy savings), implicitly used a discount rate of 25 percent in their decisions—much higher than market returns on other investments.[5] Another economist, Dermot Gately, in examining choices among refrigerators, found implicit discount rates as high as 300 percent.[6] Experimental evidence shows that there is a tendency for dynamic inconsistency in the discount rates people apply, with high rates of discount applied to the near future and lower rates for the more distant future. One way to look at it is that people tend to spend more than they planned.

Others have claimed evidence of inconsistency across countries in discount rates. It has been argued that the rate of discount or cost of capital has been much higher in the United States than it has been in Japan (at least until the spectacular drop in Japanese stock prices and land prices since the end of the 1990s). Economists Albert Ando and Alan Auerbach, as well as Robert McCauley and Steven Zimmer, made estimates of the cost of capital in the two countries based on data on earnings-price ratios, with corrections for depreciation accounting differences. They concluded that the pre-tax U.S. cost of capital has consistently exceeded the Japanese cost of capital for nonfinancial corporations over the past decade.[7]

This alleged lower cost of capital in Japan applies only to risky or speculative assets, as real interest rates on government debt have not been consistently lower there. The appearance of lower cost of capital on equity in Japan may be misleading; the high Japanese stock prices recently may not have been because of low discount rates but instead because of high expectations for future earnings. Surveys comparing American and Japanese institutional investors show that the latter have been much more optimistic about earnings growth in their country.[8] Still, such optimism, like low discount rates, may encourage saving and investment.

It is quite likely that these differences in discount rates, across economic contexts and across countries, are evidence of a general irrational inconsistency in rates of discount, and that this inconsistency is observed through time as well. There may thus be times when people attach more value (relatively) to future income from investments, and so discount rates are high, and times when they attach less value (relatively) to future income from investments. There are times when society in general is impressed with the importance of investment vehicles, when the value of such investments is receiving much popular attention, and times when public attention is attracted elsewhere. This inconsistency through time in rates of discount may thus be a source of some of the volatility we observe in prices of speculative assets.

## DISCOUNT RATES AND SAVING RATES • 99

Bull markets may sometimes be started by a change in basic opinions or values, in which personal investment vehicles are thought to be important in planning for the future; busts may sometimes occur when people feel that they shouldn't or needn't worry so much about the future. Such sources of booms and busts are not so commonly mentioned, because it is hard to get concrete proof of these sources, and because there are many other more tangible impacts (world events, federal reserve policy, economic recessions) that distract public discussion from recognizing the more subtle (and sometimes more powerful) psychological effects on the stock market.

Speculative behavior by some investors, if it has the effect of increasing the volatility of the stock market, could have the effect of raising the rate of return that other investors require before they are induced to hold stocks. The risk that is created by the speculative behavior, in effect, may displace these investors and put a "risk premium" on the discount rate used to convert expected future cash flows into today's price. Bradford De Long, J. Bradford, Andrei Shleifer, Lawrence Summers, and Robert J. Waldman have provided a theory of such effects on the discount rate.[9] This uncertainty about the effects on market prices of the erratic behavior of other investors is another cause, apart from the impatience that Pigou referred to, of discount rates that are too high.

## DO WE SAVE TOO LITTLE?

Many have argued that people left to their own devices will not save enough. Moral admonitions to save more go back long before Pigou, even to biblical times. Are people making errors in not saving more, in not buying more stocks and bonds, and other investments? Concern with inadequate national saving has gone by many names—for example, concern with a "capital shortage."[10] While tax incentives have been set up to encourage saving and investment—such things as individual retirement accounts, Keogh plans, and investment tax credits—it remains to be seen whether these measures have gone far enough.

There is every reason to expect that saving behavior may account for a substantial amount of the differences we observe in the wealth of nations. Some nations do save more than others, and the logical consequence of this saving behavior is the accumulation of wealth. Economists N. Gregory Mankiw, David Romer, and David Weil made inter-country comparisons of saving rates for the non-oil-producing countries of the world (oil-producing countries were excluded because they may attribute their economic status to a natural resource rather than to saving behavior). They found that 59 percent of the inter-country differences in gross domestic product per capita could be explained with just two variables: the percent of gross domestic product that is saved and invested (this variable had a positive effect) and the rate of population growth (this variable had an effect roughly equal to, but with the opposite sign of, the investment effect).[11]

In the United States, many of the arguments that people should be saving more amount to comparisons with the saving rate of Americans in the past or with that of other countries today. The United States had a very low saving rate in the 1980s. According to calculations by economists Alan Auerbach and Laurence Kotlikoff, which correct for some biases in the usual saving measures due to inflation and asymmetric treatment of dividends and capital gains, the U.S. private saving rate (the fraction of private sector disposable income not consumed by households) averaged only 6.7 percent in the years 1985–88, compared with 11.1 percent in 1970–79 and 11.2 percent 1960–69.[12] The *national* saving rate differs from the private saving rate in that it includes government saving as well; government saving has been diminished in the past decade by the federal budget deficit. Auerbach and Kotlikoff, correcting personal saving by including as personal saving an estimate of consumer durable purchases, and correcting government saving by including as government saving an investment component of government expenditure, estimated the national saving rate at only 7.1 percent in 1985, compared with 11.8 percent in 1970–79 and 13.0 percent in 1960–69.

Comparisons of American saving with the saving rate in Japan have been widely cited; the Japanese appear to save much more, and this higher saving rate is interpreted as part of the postwar Japanese success story. But the disparity between Japanese and U.S. saving rates is not quite as wide as commonly assumed. The economist Fumio Hayashi points out that differences in methods of national income accounting techniques between the two countries cause Japanese saving to be relatively overstated.[13] Japanese national income accounts use historical cost depreciation estimates, rather than the replacement costs estimates used in the United States. In inflationary periods, historical cost depreciation tends to be a downward-biased measure of replacement costs. Moreover, Japanese national income accounts include a component of government expenditures as government saving; the U.S. accounts do not.

Hayashi computed adjusted Japanese saving rates, using accounting techniques comparable to those in the United States. With his adjustments, Japanese national saving rates (that is, government and private savings as a percentage of net national product) have not been uniformly higher than U.S. national saving rates; U.S. saving rates were higher than Japanese saving rates in the mid-1950s and, briefly, in the late 1970s. Still, even with his adjusted estimates, Japanese saving rates show a marked tendency to exceed those in the United States; his adjusted national saving rate for Japan in 1987 was more than twice the saving rate of the United States in the same year.

These differences through time and across countries are not fully explained by theories of rational economic behavior. One might think that the changes in saving rates in the United States might be explained in terms of the demographic changes associated with the "baby boom." But Auerbach and Kotlikoff conclude that postwar changes in U.S. saving rates are not well explained by such demographics.[14] (They do argue that savings may soon stage a partial comeback in the United States, as more of the baby-boom generation enter their middle age, during which both income and saving tend to be high.)

Why then has the U.S. national saving rate declined so much? The economist B. Douglas Bernheim argues that the decline in saving in the United States since the 1960s might be explained in part by two psychological phenomena.[15] The first is a change in culture associated with the relative decline in the population of individuals who experienced the economic traumas of the depression of the 1930s. He asserts that "the longest peacetime expansion on record has promoted a false sense of security and stability."[16] The second is an increase in the percent of personal income accounted for by interest income—an increase associated with the national shift from equity toward debt finance. He believes that people may feel more free to spend interest income.

Why has Japan in recent decades had so much higher saving rates than the United States and so much higher saving rates than in its own history? Lawrence J. Christiano argues against Hayashi's assertion that the high saving rates in Japan in the post-World War II period were caused by the rational desire to rebuild the capital stock destroyed during the war; such a theory would not explain either the high saving rates today (long after the war) or the relatively low Japanese saving rates right after the war.[17] An attractive alternative explanation for the high rate of Japanese saving may be that it is just the result of the high postwar growth of Japanese national income. Japanese saving was high in the 1970s, when national income was growing the fastest.

Japanese savers may not behave any differently than American savers in similar circumstances; American savers in the past few decades have not experienced such high growth rates of income in comparison with Japan. At a time of rapidly growing income, there may be a general tendency for people to save more, if they adapt their expenditures only sluggishly to the increased income or if they hold off on increasing expenditures because they do not really believe that the income growth is real (for example, that it is more than a temporary aberration). This theory does not fit perfectly; the periods of high savings in Japan have not corresponded closely to periods of high growth in national income in Japan.

Other factors that may have played some role in promoting the high savings rate in Japan in the past few decades are Japan's slowness in developing a home mortgage market combined with the high price of housing (so people needed to save a great deal for their housing), Japan's relative slowness in developing an adequate social security system (so people had more reason to worry about whether their savings would be adequate), and Japan's relatively favorable tax treatment in the past for capital income (so people could anticipate more rewards from their saving).

Bernheim doubts that any of these explanations is adequate to explain most of the high postwar Japanese savings, and offers some different, more socially based explanations.[18] After World War II, the Japanese government launched a national campaign to promote saving, and this campaign was accompanied by marketing efforts by private financial institutions to promote saving, which suggested investments for most people. Also, the common practice among Japanese employers of paying substantial semiannual bonuses meant that a substantial fraction of employees' income was paid in lump sums, which, because people regard them differently from other income, may be easier (psychologically) to save. Advertising campaigns by Japanese banks and other financial institutions promoted plans to save the bonuses.

Apparently, savings behavior is determined largely by cultural and social factors that are beyond the scope of economic models. There is ample evidence that individual saving is not determined rationally. For example, it has been shown that lifetime consumption profiles (the patterns of consumption expenditure through time) resemble lifetime income profiles, which suggests that people do not use saving as they should to smooth out the effect of fluctuations in income on their consumption.[19] Moreover, people with higher pension benefits do not save less (as economic theory of rational actors would prescribe) than people with lower pension benefits.[20] Similarly, homeowners do not save less in assets (other than their homes) than do renters.[21] There are many other anomalies of saving behavior.[22]

Many advisers have tried to advise people from being wrongly influenced by such psychological factors by proposing how much people ought to be saving. Martin Feldstein, for example, has made a case for more savings in the United States. He makes an argument for higher saving by noting the disparity between the growth of our well-being (as measured by per capita consumption) and the growth that would be possible if there were more saving. He notes that the rate of growth of real per capita consumption in the United States has been only 2 percent a year over the past century, despite much higher average returns on financial investments.[23] Given the available return to investments in financial assets, the growth rate of consumption should be much higher. Consumption should grow at such a rate that the "marginal utility" of consumption should decline rapidly through time; only then have people exploited the profit opportunity. At a 2 percent growth rate, he argues, there cannot be much decline in the marginal utility of consumption from year to year, so people must be missing a bet by not investing more in the stock market.

This analysis disregards the risk involved in corporate investments. But such risk is apparently not large, given the low covariance of changes in real per capita consumption expenditures with changes in the value of the stock market.[24] (The low covariance means that aggregate real consumption in the United States shows little response to changes in the stock market.) Given this low covariance, people cannot have been affected much by the risk of stock market fluctuations. That the average return on stocks is so high relative to the yield on short-term debt has been called the "equity premium puzzle."[25]

Simple exercises may help us to understand whether we are saving enough. For example, consider a parent, age thirty, who decides to put $3,000 per year into a trust fund for a child and to continue doing so every year until retirement at age sixty-five. If the after-tax real (inflation corrected) rate of return is 6 percent (roughly the average after-tax real return on corporate stocks, given that capital gains are not taxed until realized), then the trust fund could yield an after-tax real income, starting the year the parent retires, of $21,000 per year *in perpetuity* for the child, the child's child, and on and on; enough to support them without further work forever. To a substantial extent, the much discussed wealth of Japan and other countries with high saving rates must be the result of having done just this over the past thirty-five years.[26] The potential benefits for one's children occur despite the fact that the government has imposed, not incentives or bounties for saving, but taxes on interest income. If the government allowed the interest contributions to the trust fund to be tax deductible, and did not tax income received by the children from the trust fund, then we might use an interest rate of 8 percent for our calculations. Then, in our example, the income of the children would be $46,000 per year in perpetuity.

Arguments that saving should be encouraged by the government beyond eliminating tax distortions that discourage saving have been criticized as authoritarian or contrary to the democratic principles on which we rely. Critics say that if people themselves do not wish to save and invest more, the government should not intervene: If people do not wish to provide bequests to their children, then that is their business and not the government's. As the economist Stephen Marglin put it, in response to Pigou:

> I for one do not accept the Pigovian formulation of social welfare . . . I want the government's social welfare function to reflect only the preferences of present individuals. Whatever else democratic theory may or may not imply, I consider it axiomatic that a democratic government reflects only the preferences of the individuals who are presently members of the body politic . . . I certainly would allow an educational role for government, including the education of today's citizens to the "rightful claims" of future generations. But education is not my reading of Pigou's policy prescription; his argument suggests intervention, not education.[27]

But it may not be possible for the government to educate all people to avoid the judgment errors that Pigou and others have described. The decisions for savings and bequests are, as noted above, apparently not well thought out by individuals, and so it is not necessarily possible for them all to learn to behave optimally in saving behavior.

Measures by the government to promote saving (and lower discount rates) might be judged as analogous to the government mandating warnings of health hazards on bottles of liquor or on packages of cigarettes, and putting taxes on these to discourage their use. Or they may be viewed as self-control mechanisms: people may elect congressmen who will enact laws that promote saving as a way of preventing themselves from making mistakes.

**Chapter Seven**

# Conclusion: Sorting Through an Array of Policy Options

There appear to be some tendencies, related to the characteristic behavior of investors and to the institutional setting in which they find themselves, for investors to trade more frequently than is really warranted in response to information about the securities they have, and to trade largely in anticipation of each others' trades. As a result, managers of firms whose shares are traded find themselves operating under wrong incentives (making decisions in light of anticipated effects on the market, rather than on the true value of their company) and securities' prices are often removed from their true value, causing costly and unnecessary disruptions in the economy. We could do without such dramatic stock market booms and crashes.

Managers of firms whose shares are traded might devote more attention to the enhancement of the true value of their firms if the shares in their firms were held for many years by the same investors. Also, managers would be less likely to think that they can get away with deceptive practices that may improve share price at the expense of long-run value. In turn, longer-term investors would not be distracted by what they think will be the effect of managers' policies on the market; they would likely be concerned instead about what the policies mean for the stream of earnings they have a claim on. These investors would be more likely to conclude that it is worthwhile to learn deeply about the operations of the companies in which they have invested, rather than glean only enough information to deal with the concerns of potential buyers of their shares the following year.

The likely effects of speculative short-term trading on financial markets are easily illustrated by analogy to the housing market. Imagine that the nation's single-family houses were largely owned and rented out by institutions that traded these houses every year. Isn't it likely, under such circumstances, that potential long-term problems that should be dealt with immediately (rotting beams under the shingles, lead-based paint, or declining quality of neighborhood public schools) would tend to be neglected? If it is believed that the next buyer is likely to be unaware of these problems or to value them improperly, wouldn't decisions to correct these problems be deferred? At the same time, might not there be certain overinvestments—say, in painting or sprucing up the houses—that give the appearance that the houses are well cared for? If our housing markets were like this, wouldn't it then be a good idea to consider changes in our institutions or incentives to encourage longer-term holding?

If there are policy measures that could be taken by the government or self-regulatory organizations to encourage longer-term holding and to reduce the impact of short-term speculation without imposing substantial other costs on society, such measures ought to be undertaken.

Given the costs imposed by financial speculation, it would seem logical to impose taxes on those who speculate to discourage short-term excessive speculation. Since the government must raise revenue, and since any feasible tax has a built-in disincentive against activities that raise that tax bite, there would seem to be no clear reason *not* to tax speculative activities. Why is it, then, that the government does not put a tax on speculative activity in financial markets but does put a very high tax on other forms of gambling, such as lotteries? The answer is supposed to be that speculative activity fulfills an economic need, whereas lotteries are pure entertainment. But the difference between financial speculation and pure gambling does not justify placing a zero tax on one and a high tax on the other.

Direct measures—such as taxes—aimed at discouraging speculation do, however, carry definite risks. The effects of other major publicly proposed policy measures to deal with excessive speculation are very uncertain, and it is even possible that they will *increase* speculation-induced price volatility.

It appears to be impossible to tax—or otherwise discourage—harmful speculative behavior *directly*. One cannot impose a tax on just those people who buy or sell stocks for purely speculative motives or as the result of theories of how other people will buy or sell stocks. The tax authorities cannot reliably distinguish them from other people who have "good" reason for buying or selling. Nor can tax authorities reliably distinguish those speculators who are helping to keep prices close to their true investment value from those who are effectively moving them away.

Any government policy measures aimed at discouraging speculative trading (such as transaction taxes, capital gains taxes with holding-period requirements, the short-short rule, or margin requirements) are blunt measures, which might work by reducing the number or the kinds of people trying to make speculative profits. But while these policy measures might promote the cause intended by their framers, they might just possibly do the opposite of what is intended—moving prices even further from where efficient markets would put them. Even many years after they are instituted, one will not be able to say with any assurance whether these measures were helpful. And even if they are determined to have been helpful at one time in history, they may become unhelpful at other times, as the characteristics or beliefs of the players who are discouraged from the taxed or restricted activities change. The theoretical arguments for—and against—these measures are not well developed. Nor is it feasible to conduct controlled experiments on a scale that would give convincing empirical evidence. When such measures were enacted, it was without much informed discussion at all—just enlightened guesswork.

I have stressed here that speculative behavior is an intellectual process, not a knee-jerk or reflexive action. People spend considerable time and thought trying to predict what the market will do, and they act with purpose. Policy measures that discourage trade to reduce speculation will be greeted by investors as obstacles to get around in their efforts to maximize returns on their portfolios. These policy measures may lead investors to de-emphasize speculative considerations when they buy and sell, but this outcome is not assured.

Still, despite the uncertain effects on speculation-induced price movements, measures to encourage longer-term holding of securities probably do encourage a more long-term horizon for the management of businesses. For example, the low turnover in single-family homes has encouraged owners to take careful account of the true long-term value of their investments.

Many have argued that national policies to discourage speculation ought to focus on institutional investors and the new derivative instruments such as stock index futures. It is true that these investors and markets are of increasing importance, and policymakers will have to be attentive to them. But there is no persuasive evidence that the growing importance of institutional investors and the trend toward increasing development of derivative markets have made the problems of excessive or destabilizing speculation any worse. These trends need not encourage greater destabilizing speculation or short-termism; it could be the opposite. Indeed, since today's institutional investors are more professional and more aware of how to think about the long term, one would think that professional investors with more markets at their disposal might do a better job of "long-term" investing than the investors of years ago.

Discouraging trade may also reduce one of the protections speculative markets provide to naive investors: to the extent that financial markets actually are efficient, the price of each asset is basically fair. This reduction of protections would be especially the case if the traders who are discouraged are, as in Senator Kassebaum's bill, investment professionals. When all prices are fair, it does not matter what a naive investor buys or sells, or when he or she buys or sells. Short-run or idiosyncratic price discrepancies tend to be eliminated very efficiently by investment professionals, even if they do not reduce the vulnerability of the economy to booms and crashes.

Policy measures to reduce excessive speculative behavior might take forms other than direct discouragement of speculative trading. We have seen that there are many proposed measures that might have the effect of encouraging long-term relationship investing by institutions, encouraging participation in governance. These measures include changing proxy rules, encouraging investor communication, and discouraging extremes of portfolio diversification for institutional investors. Such changes might be suggested by looking at institutions in other countries. Still, it is not a simple matter to conclude from such observations how we should change our institutions to make them more conducive to efficient long-term investing. We should not make the mistake of assuming that the higher growth rates in Japan or Western Germany in recent decades are due to the fact that their financial institutions are different; there are many possible causes for the high growth rates.

Other measures might help encourage a longer-term horizon by corporate managers. Jacobs has proposed that bonus incentive systems for managers be tied to longer-term—say, five-year—returns on companies' stock.[1] Thus, bonuses would be given possibly after the executive has left the company. Such an idea must sound absurd to conventional economists, who believe that stock prices are completely efficient—so that there is no conflict between maximizing five-year returns and one-year returns. But as we have seen, the pure efficient-market theory of stock prices appears to be wrong.

Others have proposed that corporations not be required to report earnings as often as they do, so that managers will not be distracted by quarter-to-quarter numbers. This idea also must sound absurd to conventional economists, who perceive people as perfectly rational optimizers who could only benefit from more frequent information reporting. But recent research on human psychology has shown that people *are* affected by apparently superficial changes in presentation or information; psychologists refer to "framing effects" (differing results depending on how questions are framed) and also to the effects of the manner in which targets are suggested.[2]

Concerns about the separation of ownership and control are inherently tied up with concerns over the effects of hostile takeovers of companies, the speculative price moves engendered by these, and the disruptions sometimes caused. Managements of firms threatened by hostile takeovers commonly argue that the takeovers are only in the short-term interests of the stockholders themselves.

Hostile takeovers sometimes are followed by an abrogation of trust or breach of implicit contract to other stakeholders in the corporation. After such takeovers, employees and other stakeholders may feel that their companies are serving the purposes of distant financial dealmakers who care nothing about them. One result may be a gradual decline in employee effectiveness; employees' productivity will not be at its peak unless employees have a sense of purpose and shared destiny with their company. Certainly some of the recent takeovers have eroded this sense.

Recent multi-constituency laws in many states have tried to address some of the problems associated with hostile takeovers. But the laws have also created new problems, by blurring the responsibilities of managers and allowing managers of targets of hostile takeovers to entrench themselves. Some changes in these laws might be instituted to deal with these problems. The Williams Act could be amended to assure stockholders the right to consider bids for the shares in a hostile takeover. The multi-constituency laws that have replaced the directors' accountability to shareholders with a general accountability might be replaced with laws that spell out more clearly the fiduciary responsibilities of directors. The present multi-constituency laws may depart too sharply from the concept of corporations as profit-making enterprises.

Still other measures aimed at dealing with the problems caused by speculation have been proposed and put to use. The Federal Reserve, for example, has a long history of making occasional efforts to stabilize the stock market through monetary policy or margin requirements. Action by the Federal Reserve was credited with preventing the 1987 crash from worsening and the October 1989 stock market drop from developing into a full-fledged crash. The apparent intention of the Federal Reserve was to be a stabilizing influence at a time of perceived speculative panic—reducing speculative activity by encouraging belief in a more stable stock market, and reducing public perceptions of the likelihood of a speculative panic. But it would not be wise to develop these minimal gestures to stabilize markets into serious efforts to stabilize markets on a regular basis; they should be reserved for times of great crisis, when the market may look to the Federal Reserve for leadership.

In addition to the above-mentioned measures, which deal directly with the problems of speculation, and the separation of management from the financial markets, there are some other policy steps that might be taken to help resolve the basic problems discussed.

As discussed above, the problem of short-termism may be directly related not only to the issue of speculation, but also to a long-run real rate of discount for equities that is too high, or to a rate of national saving that is too low. It was argued above that there are ample grounds not to adopt a laissez-faire attitude to these matters; that individual decisionmaking that ultimately determines discount rates or saving rates may not be optimal. Our legislators may wish to enact policies that lower the cost of capital to corporations (for example, by cutting the corporate profits tax).[3] Or they may wish to encourage saving among individuals (for example, by tax breaks for saving). Doing these things may well boost investments of all sorts—including investment in research and development that so many are concerned about today.

It should also be borne in mind that much of the benefits of research and development to society are public goods that accrue to everyone. As such, there tends to be underinvestment in research in development. This problem has long been recognized, and accounts for government support of basic research in the sciences and government provision of patents and licenses. It may be wise policy to extend such support. For example, government might increase its support for research in product development or marketing—so long as the research has been judged to provide a potential public benefit.

In addition, the government might also subsidize financial research and try thereby to encourage greater professionalization of professional investors. Since much financial research is perceived as a public good, that too tends to be undersupplied. The profession of investing today in many ways resembles that of the medical profession one hundred years ago—with much research being secret and proprietary, and with much quackery going unexposed. Investment professionals should be encouraged to think that what they do benefits the country, and that they are therefore under some moral obligation to review their research publicly and to let the truth be known. Developing more of a public recognition that this profession has some scientific and moral authority may be an important means of reducing purely speculative price movements.

# Notes

## CHAPTER ONE

1. See, for example, Mark L. Mitchell and Jeffrey M. Netter, "Triggering the 1987 Stock Market Crash: Antitakeover Provisions in the Proposed House Ways and Means Tax Bill?" *Journal of Financial Economics* 24 (1989), pp. 37–68.

2. Richard B. Hoey, David Rolley, and Helen Hotchkiss, *Decision-Makers' Poll* (New York: Drexel Burnham Lambert, Inc., 1988).

3. Data are courtesy of Blue Chip Economic Indicators, Eggert Economic Enterprises, Sedona Arizona.

4. See Gerard Gennotte and Hayne Leland, "Market Liquidity, Hedging, and Crashes," *American Economic Review* 80, December 1990, pp. 999–1021; Charles Jacklin, Allan W. Kleidon, and Paul Pfleiderer, "Underestimation of Portfolio Insurance and the Crash of October, 1987," Working Paper No. 1098, Graduate School of Business, Stanford University, 1990; and Sanford J. Grossman, "Insurance Seen and Unseen: The Impact on Markets," *Journal of Portfolio Management*, Summer 1988, pp. 5–8.

5. Robert J. Shiller, *Market Volatility* (Cambridge, Mass.: MIT Press, 1989).

6. See, for example, Karl E. Case, "The Market For Single Family Homes in Boston," *New England Economic Review* (1986), pp. 125–37; and Karl E. Case and Robert J. Shiller, "The Behavior of Home Buyers in Boom and Post-Boom Markets," *New England Economic Review* (1988), pp. 29–46.

7. John M. Keynes, *The General Theory of Employment, Interest, and Money* (New York: Harbinger, 1964). (First published in 1936.)

8. Benjamin Graham and David L. Dodd, *Security Analysis* (New York: McGraw-Hill Book Company, 1934), p. 52.

9. J. Stein, "Efficient Capital Markets, Inefficient Firms: A Model of Myopic Corporate Behavior," *Quarterly Journal of Economics* 104 (November 1989), pp. 655–69. See also, Stewart Myers, "Signalling and Accounting Information," National Bureau of Economic Research Working Paper No. 3193,

112 ◆ WHO'S MINDING THE STORE?

December 1989; and Andrei Shleifer and Robert Vishny, "Equilibrium Short Horizons of Investors and Firms," *American Economic Review* 80 (May 1990), pp. 148–53.

10. See Kenneth A. Froot, Andre F. Perold, and Jeremy C. Stein, "Shareholder Trading Practices and Corporate Investment Horizons," National Bureau of Economic Research Working Paper No. 3638, March 1991.

## CHAPTER TWO

1. "Tax on Certain Trades by Pension Funds is Considered by Senate Finance Chief," *The Wall Street Journal*, September 20, 1989.

2. Felix Rohatyn, "Institutional 'Investor' or Speculator," *The Wall Street Journal*, June 24, 1988, op-ed page.

3. Nancy L. Kassebaum, "How About Taxing Pension Fund Profits?" *The New York Times*, August 30, 1989, p. A23.

4. Louis Lowenstein, *What's Wrong with Wall Street* (Reading, Mass.: Addison Wesley, 1988), p. 11.

5. James Tobin, "On the Efficiency of the Financial System," *Lloyds Bank Review*, July 1984, p. 10.

6. "Litmus Test in Pennsylvania Anti-Takeover Law," *The New York Times*, April 19, 1990, p. D7.

7. See, for example, Robert Eisenberger, *Blue Monday: The Loss of the Work Ethic in America* (New York: Paragon House, 1989).

8. See, for example, Daniel Yankelovich and John Immerwahr, *Putting the Work Ethic to Work: A Public Agenda Report on Restoring America's Competitive Vitality*, Public Agenda Foundation, 1983 or Joani Nelson-Horchler, "Are U.S. Workers Lazy?" *Industry Week*, June 10, 1985, pp. 45–52.

9. William C. McGowan, "The Hustle-Butt Society," *Business and Society Review*, Spring 1987, pp. 52–53.

## CHAPTER THREE

1. William F. Sharpe, *Investments*, 3rd Edition (Englewood Cliffs, N.J.: Prentice Hall, 1985), p. 67.

2. M. Kallick, D. Suits, T. Dielman, and J. Hybels, *A Survey of American Gambling Attitudes and Behavior* (Ann Arbor: Survey Research Center Institute for Social Research, University of Michigan, 1975).

3. Benjamin Graham and David L. Dodd, *Security Analysis* (New York: McGraw-Hill Book Company, 1934).

4. Muzafer Sherif, "An Experimental Approach to the Study of Attitudes," *Sociometry* 1 (1937), pp. 90–98.

5. William J. McGuire, "The Nature of Attitudes and Attitude Change," in Garner Lindzey and Elliot Aronson, eds., *Handbook of Social Psychology* (Redding, Mass.: Addison Wesley, 1969), p. 231.

## NOTES • 113

6. For example, see Stuart Oskamp, "Overconfidence in Case-Study Judgments," *The Journal of Consulting Psychology* 29 (1965), pp. 261–65, reprinted in Daniel Kahneman, Paul Slovic, and Amos Tversky, *Judgment Under Uncertainty: Heuristics and Biases* (Cambridge: Cambridge University Press, 1982).

7. New York Stock Exchange, *Market Volatility and Investor Confidence: Report to the Board of Director of the New York Stock Exchange, Inc.*, New York, 1990.

8. Ibid., p. B3-3.

9. See Eugene F. Fama, "The Behavior of Stock Market Prices," *Journal of Business*, 38 (1965), p. 94, and Eugene F. Fama, "Efficient Capital Markets: A Review of Empirical Work," *Journal of Finance* 24 (1970), pp. 383–417.

10. George R. Gibson, *The Stock Exchanges of London, Paris, and New York* (New York: G. P. Putnam and Sons, 1889), p. 11.

11. John T. Flynn, *Security Speculation: Its Economic Effects* (New York: Harcourt, Brace & Co., 1934), pp. 127–28.

12. Eugene F. Fama, "Efficient Capital Markets: A Review of Empirical Work," *Journal of Finance* 24 (1970), pp. 383–417.

13. See Robert J. Shiller, "Do Stock Prices Move Too Much to Be Justified by Subsequent Movements in Dividends?" *American Economic Review* 36 (1981), pp. 291–304, reprinted in R. Shiller, *Market Volatility* (Cambridge, Mass.: MIT Press, 1989); Stephen F. LeRoy and Richard D. Porter, "The Present Value Relation: Tests Based on Variance Bounds," *Econometrica* 49 (1981), pp. 555–574.

14. See Werner DeBondt and Richard Thaler, "Does the Stock Market Overreact?" *Journal of Finance* 39 (1985), pp. 793–805.

15. James M. Poterba and Lawrence H. Summers, "Mean Reversions in Stock Prices: Evidence and Implications," *Journal of Financial Economics* 22 (1988), pp. 26–59.

16. See Eugene F. Fama and Kenneth R. French, "Dividend Yields and Expected Stock Returns," *Journal of Financial Economics* 22 (1988), pp. 3–25; Eugene F. Fama and Kenneth R. French, "Permanent and Temporary Components of Stock Prices," *Journal of Political Economy* 96 (1988), pp. 246–73.

17. For further discussion of some of these studies, see Shiller, *Market Volatility*; Lawrence H. Summers, "Does the Stock Market Rationally Reflect Fundamental Values?" *Journal of Finance* 41 (1986), pp. 591–601; Kenneth West, "Bubbles, Fads, and Stock Price Volatility Tests: A Partial Evaluation," *Journal of Finance* 43 (1988), pp. 648–50; or Paul H. Kupiec, "Do Stock Prices Exhibit Excess Volatility, Frequently Deviate from Fundamental Values, and Generally Behave Inefficiently? If So, Can Anything Be Done about It?" (reproduced), Board of Governors of the Federal Reserve System, 1992.

18. Milton Friedman argued that profitable speculation will always be stabilizing and that destabilizing speculation will always be unprofitable. See Milton Friedman, *Essays in Positive Economics* (Chicago: University of Chicago Press, 1953). Thus, there is no need to provide any government interference or subsidy to efforts to stabilizing markets. Friedman's assertion has been

challenged by a number of economic theorists: William Baumol, "Speculation, Profitability and Stability," *Review of Economics and Statistics* 39 (1957), p. 263; M. J. Farrell, "Profitable Speculation," *Economica* 33 (1966), pp. 183–93; Meir Kohn, "Competitive Speculation," *Econometrica* 46 (September 1978), pp. 1061–76; Oliver Hart and David Kreps, "Price Destabilizing Speculation," *Journal of Political Economy* 94 (1986), pp. 927–52; Jeremy G. Stein, "Informational Externalities and Welfare-Reducing Speculation," *Journal of Political Economy* 95 (1987), pp. 1123–25. These challenges seem to rely on some restrictive assumptions (for example, a small number of imperfectly competitive speculators) and have not decisively refuted Friedman's claim.

19. Olivier Blanchard and Mark Watson, "Bubbles, Rational Expectations, and Financial Markets," in Paul Wachtel, ed., *Crises in the Economic and Financial Structure* (1981); J. Tirole, "Asset Bubbles and Overlapping Generations," *Econometrica* 53 (1985), p. 1499; B. Diba and H. Grossman, "Rational Bubbles in Stock Prices?" National Bureau of Economic Research Working Paper No. 1779, 1985; and Kenneth West, "Bubbles, Fads, and Stock Price Volatility Tests: A Partial Evaluation," *Journal of Finance* 43 (1988), pp. 648–50.

20. Frank Knight, *Risk Uncertainty and Profit* (New York: Houghton Mifflin, 1921).

21. Ibid., p. 232.

22. Robert J. Shiller, "Market Volatility and Investor Behavior," *American Economic Review Papers and Proceedings*, May 1990.

23. See David M. Cutler, James M. Poterba, and Lawrence H. Summers, "What Moves Stock Prices?" *Journal of Portfolio Management* 15, no. 3 (Spring 1989), pp. 4–12.

24. Robert J. Shiller and William J. Feltus, "Fear of a Crash Caused the Crash," *The New York Times*, October 29, 1989.

25. David Scharfstein and Jeremy Stein provide a theory that in equilibriums with fully rational investors arbitrary focal points may play a role, as investors mimic the concerns of other investors. David S. Scharfstein and Jeremy C. Stein, "Herd Behavior and Investment," *American Economic Review* 80, no. 3 (June 1990), pp. 465–79.

26. Robert W. Kolb and Ricardo J. Rodriguez have documented that, from 1962 to 1985, on Friday the 13ths, the U.S. stock market tended to decline slightly, despite the fact that on other Fridays the market tended to rise strongly. See Robert W. Kolb and Ricardo J. Rodriguez, "Friday the Thirteenth: 'Part VII'—A Note," *Journal of Finance* 62, no. 5 (December 1987), pp. 1385–87.

27. Robert J. Shiller, "Speculative Prices and Popular Models," *Journal of Economic Perspectives* 4, no. 2 (Spring 1990), pp. 55–65.

28. Robert J. Shiller, "Stock Prices and Social Dynamics," *Brookings Papers on Economic Activity* 2 (1984), pp. 457–98 (reprinted in Robert J. Shiller, *Market Volatility*).

29. All U.S. surveys of institutional investors reported in this background paper were based on random samples from the alphabetical index

of investment managers in the *Money Market Directory of Pension Funds and Their Investment Managers* (New York: McGraw-Hill, various dates). The survey of individual investors was based on a random sample from the continental United States of individuals whose income was predicted to be over $99,900 per year; the sample was produced by Survey Sampling, Inc. Robert J. Shiller, Fumiko Kon-Ya, and Yoshiro Tsutsui, "Speculative Behavior in the Stock Markets: Evidence from the United States and Japan" (reproduced), Yale University, 1990.

30. Lawrence H. Summers and Victoria P. Summers, "When Financial Markets Work Too Well: A Cautious Case for a Securities Transactions Tax," *Journal of Financial Services Research* 3 (December 1989), pp. 261–86.

31. See Amar Bhide, "Active Markets, Deficient Governance" (reproduced), Harvard Business School, 1991; Louis Lowenstein, *What's Wrong with Wall Street* (Reading, Mass.: Addison Wesley, 1988).

## CHAPTER FOUR

1. Carolyn Kay Brancato and Patrick A. Gaughan, "The Growth of Institutional Investors in U.S. Capital Markets" (reproduced), Institutional Investor Project, Columbia Center for Law and Economic Studies, 1988, p. 13.

2. Economic Planning Agency (Keizai Kikakucho), government of Japan, *Financial System in a Time of Reform* (Henkakuki no kin'yu sisutemu), June 1989, Table 1. These figures for Japan are corrected for cross-holding of stocks by Japanese firms. That is, what is reported here is the proportion of institutional holdings divided by one minus the proportion of business corporation holdings of equity. This corrected figure gives a better measure of the proportion of institutional ownership of equity, since the business corporation holdings of equity are themselves indirectly owned by the shareholders of the business corporation with the holdings.

3. New York Stock Exchange, *Fact Book*, 1989, p. 73.

4. Louis Lowenstein, statement before the Subcommittee on Domestic Monetary Policy, Committee on Banking, Finance, and Urban Affairs, U.S. House of Representatives, May 17, 1988.

5. Economic Planning Agency, *Financial System in a Time of Reform*, Table 4a.

6. It should be noted that it is not strictly accurate to attribute high turnover to institutional investors as a group. Institutional investors are not all alike. Some kinds of institutional investors (bank trust departments and insurance companies) have turnover well below the market average, and some individual firms show extremely low turnover. See Carolyn Kay Brancato, "Institutional Investors and Corporate America: Conflicts and Resolutions: An Overview of the Role of Institutional Investors in Capital Markets and corporate Governance," in *Impact of Institutional investors on Corporate Governance, Takeovers, and the Capital Markets*, hearing before the Subcommittee

on Securities of the Committee on Banking, Housing and Urban Affairs, United States Senate (Washington, D.C.: U.S. Government Printing Office, 1990), exhibit 17, pp. 70–85.

7. Kenneth A. Froot, Andre F. Perold, and Jeremy C. Stein, "Shareholder Trading Practices and Corporate Investment Horizons," National Bureau of Economic Research, Working Paper No. 3638, March 1991.

8. Nancy L. Kassebaum, "How About Taxing Pension Fund Profits?" *The New York Times*, August 30, 1989, p. A23.

9. Charles Leadbeater, "Short Term Pressure Curbs Ruled Out," *Financial Times*, June 26, 1990, p. 10. The term "the City" is the British equivalent of "Wall Street."

10. U.S. Securities and Exchange Commission, The Office of Economic Analysis, "Institutional Ownership, Tender Offers, and Long-Term Investments," Washington, D.C., April 19, 1985.

11. John J. McConnell and Chris J. Muscarella, "Corporate Capital Expenditure Decisions and the Market Value of the Firm," *Journal of Financial Economics* 14, no. 3, September 1985, pp. 399–422; Su Han Chan, John D. Martin, and John W. Kensinger, "Corporate Research and Development Expenditures and Share Value," *Journal of Financial Economics* 26, no. 2, August 1990.

12. U.S. Securities and Exchange Commission, The Office of Economic Analysis, "Institutional Ownership, Tender Offers, and Long-Term Investments," Washington, D.C., April 19, 1985.

13. Lucian Arye Bebchuk and Lars Stole, "Do Short-Term Managerial Objectives Lead to Under- or Over-Investment in Long-Term Projects?" National Bureau of Economic Research, Technical Working Paper No. 98, March 1991.

14. "Performance Fees Make Headway," *Institutional Investor*, June 1989, pp. 129–30.

15. Financial Executives Institute, Committee on Investment of Employee Benefit Assets, "Survey of Pension Fund Investment Practices" (reproduced), 1990, p. 3.

16. William M. O'Barr and John M. Conley, *Fortune and Folly: The Wealth and Power of Institutional Investing* (Homewood, Illinois: Business One Irwin, 1992), p. 168.

17. The Confederation of British Industry asked a similar question of chief executives of two hundred United Kingdom parent companies rather than to institutional investors: They asked "Are you satisfied that financial institutions take a long-term and strategic evaluation of your company?" Of those responding, 60 percent said "yes"; 40 percent said "no." Confederation of British Industry, *Short-Termism* (reproduced), October 1987.

18. Anise Wallace, "Hiring High and Firing Low," *Institutional Investor*, September 1979, p. 54.

19. Quoted by Anise Wallace, "Hiring High and Firing Low," p. 67.

20. See William N. Goetzman and Roger G. Ibbotson, "Do Winners Repeat? Patterns in Mutual Fund Behavior" (unpublished paper), Columbia University, 1990, and Darryll Hendricks, Jayendu Patel, and Richard Zeckhauser, "Hot Hands in Mutual Funds: The Persistence of Performance, 1974–87" (unpublished paper), John F. Kennedy School of Government, Harvard University, May 1990.

21. Nancy Belliveau, "Are Pension Administrators Monitoring their Managers to Death?" *Institutional Investor*, January 1974, p. 81.

22. Irving L. Janis, *Victims of Groupthink* (Boston: Houston, 1972).

23. Adolf A. Berle, Jr., and Gardiner C. Means, *The Modern Corporation and Private Property* (New York: The Macmillan Company, 1932).

24. Robin Marris and Adrian Wood, *The Corporate Economy: Growth, Competition and Innovative Potential* (Cambridge, Mass.: Harvard University Press, 1971).

25. Brancato, "Institutional Investors and Corporate America: Conflicts and Resolutions: An Overview of the Role of Institutional Investors in Capital Markets and corporate Governance," p. 85.

26. Julie Rohrer, "The New Activism at Institutions," *Institutional Investor*, October 1983, pp. 177–97.

27. Samuel B. Graves and Sandra A. Waddock, "Ownership at a Distance: Implications of Activist Institutional Investors," *Business in the Contemporary World*, Spring 1990, pp. 83–89.

28. Brett Duval Fromson, "The Big Owners Roar," *Fortune* 122 (July 30, 1990), pp. 66–78.

29. Bernard S. Black, "The Legal and Historical Contingency of Shareholder Passivity" (reproduced), Columbia University Law School, 1990.

30. Poison pills, as adopted by individual companies, specify that if a person or group acquires beneficial ownership of more than a threshold percentage of a company's stock, other shareholders will be allowed to purchase common stock from the company at a fraction of the market price, thereby diluting the person's or group's holdings. Some pills allow companies to lower the threshold by declaring a shareholder to be an "adverse person" who intends to cause pressure contrary to the business or prospects of the company.

31. Paul Sheard calculated that the average loan share of the main bank on the first section of the Tokyo Stock Exchange in 1980 was 25 percent. The main bank is also typically a major shareholder in the firm. Sheard calculated that in 1980, the main bank was the largest or second largest shareholder in 39 percent of listed firms and among the top five shareholders in 72 percent of firms. See Paul Sheard, "The Main Bank System and Corporate Monitoring and Control in Japan," *Journal of Economic Behavior and Organization* 11 (1989), pp. 399–422. According to a survey, known as the 1989 White Paper on Shareholders Meetings, taken by the Commercial Law Center, a Tokyo Association, 69.9 percent of the 1,536 listed companies

have a majority of stock held by "friendly" shareholders. See Yuko Mizuno, "Popularity of Equity Financing Threatening 'Keiretsu' System," *Japan Economic Journal*, December 30, 1989, p. 36.

32. Louis Lowenstein, *What's Wrong with Wall Street* (Reading, Mass.: Addison Wesley, 1988).

33. Robert B. Reich, "Bailout: A Comparative Study in Law and Industrial Structure," *The Yale Journal of Regulation* 2 (1985), pp. 163–224.

34. Graves and Waddock, "Ownership at a Distance: Implications of Activist Institutional Investors," pp. 83–89.

35. Oliver E. Williamson, *Markets and Hierarchies* (New York: Free Press, 1975).

36. Robert H. Hayes and William J. Abernathy, "Managing Our Way to Economic Decline," *Harvard Business Review* 58 (July-August 1980), pp. 66–77.

37. Michael Jensen, "Eclipse of the Public Corporation," *Harvard Business Review*, September/October 1989, pp. 61–74.

38. See Frank R. Lichtenberg and Donald Siegel, "The Effects of Leveraged Buyouts on Productivity and Related Aspects of Firm Behavior," NBER Working Paper No. 3022, June 1989. Also see Steven Kaplan, "The Effects of Management Buyouts on Operating Performance and Value," *Journal of Financial Economics* 24, 1989.

39. Scott B. Smart and Joel Waldfogel, "Measuring the Effect of Restructuring on Corporate Performance: The Case of Management Buyouts" (reproduced), Indiana University, 1991.

40. Bevis Longstreth, "Takeovers, Corporate Governance, and Stock Ownership: Some Disquieting Trends," *Journal of Portfolio Management*, Spring 1990, pp. 54–59.

41. A buyer of a contract today on the S&P 500 futures market with an exercise date three months in the future is essentially making a promise to pay on the exercise date 500 times the difference between the futures price today and the S&P stock price index. However, the buyer's margin account will be debited or credited on a daily basis until the contract is closed out.

42. See Saul Hansell, "Is the World Ready for Synthetic Equity?" *Institutional Investor*, August 1990, pp. 54–61, for a description of the emerging trends in synthetic equities.

43. Jennifer Quinn, George Sofianos, and William E. Tschirhart, "Program Trading and Index Arbitrage," in *Market Volatility and Investor Confidence*, New York Stock Exchange, New York, 1990, p. F-4.

44. Kenneth A. Froot, James F. Gammil, Jr., and Andre F. Perold, "New Trading Practices and the Short-Run Predictability of the S&P 500," in *Market Volatility and Investor Confidence*, New York Stock Exchange, 1990.

45. Robert W. Kolb, *Understanding Futures Markets* (Miami, Florida: Kolb Publishing Company, 1991), pp. 138–40.

46. See, for example, A. Ronald Gallant, Peter E. Rossi, and George Tauchen, "Stock Prices and Volume," Working Paper Series on Economics and Econometrics, No. 90–82, Graduate School of Business, University of Chicago, January 1990.

47. See G. William Schwert, "Why Does Stock Market Volatility Change over Time?" *Journal of Finance* 44 (December 1989), pp. 1115–53, and G. William Schwert, "Stock Market Volatility," in *Market Volatility and Investor Confidence*, New York Stock Exchange, 1990.

## CHAPTER FIVE

1. James Tobin, "On the Efficiency of the Financial System," *Lloyds Bank Review*, July 1984, pp. 1–15; Lawrence H. Summers and Victoria P. Summers, "When Financial Markets Work Too Well: A Cautious Case for a Securities Transactions Tax," Journal of Financial Services Research, December 1989, pp. 261–86.

2. John Maynard Keynes, *The General Theory of Employment, Interest, and Money* (New York: Harbinger, 1964), p. 160. (First published in 1936.)

3. "Swedish Turnover Tax: No Puppy Love," *Banker*, December 1988.

4. It is not clear why a holding-period requirement need be attached to a capital gains tax and not a transaction tax. The seller of an asset could be taxed a fixed amount, regardless of the capital gain or loss (the amount depending on the length of time since the purchase of the asset). This would eliminate the above-noted asymmetry in the effects of capital gains taxes between up and down price movements. Perhaps the reason we do not see such transaction taxes proposed is tradition: The United States has had experience with capital gains taxes with holding-period requirements, but not with transaction taxes with holding period requirements.

5. James R. Repetti, "The Use of the Tax Law to Stabilize the Stock Market: The Efficacy of Holding Period Requirements," *Virginia Tax Review* 8, 1989, pp. 591–637.

6. Another effect of capital gains taxes, of course, will be to limit trading that is for legitimate purposes: This tax will create a locked-in effect.

7. Karl E. Case, "The Market For Single Family Homes in Boston," *New England Economic Review*, 1986, pp. 125–37; Karl E. Case and Robert J. Shiller, "The Behavior of Home Buyers in Boom and Post-Boom Markets," *New England Economic Review*, 1988, pp. 29–46.

8. Merton H. Miller, John D. Hawke, Jr., Burton Malkiel, and Myron Scholes, "Preliminary Report of the Committee of Inquiry Appointed by the Chicago Mercantile Exchange to Examine the Events Surrounding October 19, 1987" (reproduced), December 1987.

9. Gikas Hardouvelis and Steve Peristiani, "Do Margin Requirements Matter? Evidence from U.S. and Japanese Stock Markets," *Federal Reserve Bank of New York Quarterly Review*, Winter 1989/90, pp. 16–35.

10. David A. Hsieh and Merton H. Miller, "Margin Requirements and Stock Market Volatility," *Journal of Finance* 45, March 1990, pp. 3–29. Hsieh and Miller have written a detailed critique of earlier work of Gikas Hardouvelis that claims to find a negative association between margin requirements and volatility; their criticism does not extend to the results cited here.

11. Presidential Task Force on Market Mechanisms (Brady Commission), *Report* (Washington, D.C.: U.S. Government Printing Office, 1988). More recently, a special New York Stock Exchange panel recommended tighter limits for trading halts, so that the market would be closed after a 100 point drop in the Dow. See New York Stock Exchange, *Market Volatility and Investor Confidence: Report to the Board of Director of the New York Stock Exchange, Inc.,* 1990. These recommendations have not yet been implemented.

12. The New York Stock Exchange-Chicago Mercantile Exchange circuit breakers had their first tests when the limit on the S&P contract was reached on October 13 and October 24, 1989. One Securities and Exchange Commission study of these episodes concluded that there is evidence for this gravitational effect then. See Henry McMillan, "The Effects of S&P500 Futures Market Circuit Breakers on Liquidity and Price Discovery," U.S. Securities and Exchange Commission, Washington, D.C., June 24, 1990 (reproduced).

13. James B. Stewart and Daniel Hertzberg, "Terrible Tuesday: How the Stock Market Almost Disintegrated A Day After the Crash," *Wall Street Journal,* November 20, 1987, p. 1, p. 23.

14. Charles M. C. Lee, Mark Ready, and Paul J. Seguin found that the volatility of stock prices after "no-news halts" when trading was suspended without any news event was not much different from the normal volatility of stock prices. Charles M. C. Lee, Mark Ready, and Paul J. Seguin, "Volume, Volatility, and NYSE Trading Halts" (unpublished paper), University of Michigan, November 1991.

15. Louis Lowestein, *What's Wrong With Wall Street* (Reading, Mass.: Addison Wesley, 1988); Michael T. Jacobs, *Short-Term America: The Causes and Cures of Our Business Myopia* (Boston, Mass.: Harvard Business School Press, 1991).

16. Ronald J. Gilson and Reinier Kraakman, "Reinventing the Outside Director: An Agenda for Institutional Investors," *Stanford Law Review* 43 (1991), p. 863.

17. John C. Coffee, Jr., "Liquidity Versus Control: The Institutional Investor as Corporate Monitor," *Columbia Law Review* 91, no. 6 (1991), pp. 1277–1368.

18. Charles Leadbetter, "Short Term Pressure Curbs Ruled Out," *Financial Times,* June 26, 1990, p. 10.

19. See Bernard Black, "Shareholder Passivity Reexamined," *Michigan Law Review* 89 (1990), p. 520; Gilson and Kraakman, "Reinventing the Outside Director: An Agenda for Institutional Investors"; and Coffee, "Liquidity Versus Control: The Institutional Investor as Corporate Monitor."

## CHAPTER SIX

1. Discussions about whether the level of stock market prices are too low or too high are often about the likely level of future corporate earnings or dividends, about the expected future payments to shareholders, rather than about the rate of discount to be applied to these payments. Here, in contrast, we are taking the expected future dividends as given and asking whether the market discounts them too much. It is, of course, possible that the market can be too high because of overly optimistic expectations about future dividends, even if the rate of discount is too high.

2. A. C. Pigou, *Economics of Welfare* (London: Macmillan, 1934). (First published in 1920.)

3. Ibid., p. 29.

4. A survey of this research is in George Loewenstein and Richard H. Thaler, "Anomalies: Intertemporal Choice," *Journal of Economic Perspectives* 3, no. 4 (Fall 1989), pp. 181–93.

5. Jerry Hausman, "Individual Discount Rates and the Purchase and Utilization of Energy-Using Durables," *Bell Journal of Economics* 10, 1979, pp. 33–54.

6. Dermot Gately, "Individual Discount Rates and the Purchase of Energy Using Durables: Comment," *Bell Journal of Economics* 11, 1980, pp. 373–74.

7. It should be noted that in substantial measure, this low cost of capital in Japan is related to the high price (and consequent high price-to-earnings ratio) of land. The value of land held by corporations in Japan is a substantial part of the value of corporate equities. Albert Ando and Alan J. Auerbach, "The Cost of Capital in the United States and Japan: A Comparison," *Journal of Japanese and International Economies* 2, 1988, pp. 134–58; Robert N. McCauley and Steven A. Zimmer, "Explaining International Differences in the Cost of Capital," *Federal Reserve Bank of New York Quarterly Review*, Summer 1989, pp. 7–28.

8. Robert J. Shiller, Fumiko Kon-Ya, and Yoshiro Tsutsui, "Speculative Behavior in the Stock Markets: Evidence from the United States and Japan" (reproduced), Yale University, 1990.

9. Bradford De Long, J. Bradford, Andrei Shleifer, Lawrence Summers, and Robert J. Waldman, "Noise Trader Risk in Financial Markets," *Journal of Political Economy* 98, No. 4 (1990), pp. 703–38.

10. See New York Stock Exchange, *The Capital Needs and Savings Potential of the United States Economy: Projections Through 1985*, New York, September 1974; William E. Simon, Public Hearings on the Subject of Tax Reform before the Committee on Ways and Means, House of Representatives, 94th Cong., 1st sess., *Tax Reform*, pt. 5, Washington, D.C., July 31, 1975.

11. N. Gregory Mankiw, David Romer, and David N. Weil, "A Contribution to the Empirics of Economic Growth," *Quarterly Journal of Economics* 107, no. 2 (May 1992), pp. 407–37.

12. Alan Auerbach and Laurence Kotlikoff, "Demographics, Fiscal Policy, and U.S. Savings in the 1980's," National Bureau of Economic Research, Working Paper No. 3150, 1990.

13. Fumio Hayashi, "Is Japan's Saving Rate High?" *Federal Reserve Bank of Minneapolis Quarterly Review*, Spring 1989, pp. 3–9.

14. Auerbach and Kotlikoff, "Demographics, Fiscal Policy, and U.S. Savings in the 1980's."

15. B. Douglas Bernheim, *The Vanishing Nest Egg: Reflections on Saving in America*, a Twentieth Century Fund Paper (New York: Priority Press Publications, 1991).

16. Ibid., p. 80.

17. Lawrence J. Christiano, "Understanding Japan's Saving Rate: The Reconstruction Hypothesis," *Federal Reserve Bank of Minneapolis Quarterly Review*, Spring 1989, pp. 10–25.

18. Bernheim, *The Vanishing Nest Egg*.

19. See Laurence J. Kotlikoff and Lawrence H. Summers, "The Role of Intergenerational Transfers in Aggregate Capital Formation," *Journal of Political Economy* 89, 1981, pp. 706–32; Paul Courant, Edward Gramlich, and John Laitner, "A Dynamic Micro Estimate of the Life Cycle Model," in Henry J. Aaron and Gary Burtless, eds., *Retirement and Economic Behavior* (Washington D.C.: The Brookings Institution, 1986); and Chris Carroll and Lawrence H. Summers, "Consumption Growth Parallels Income Growth: Some New Evidence," Department of Economics, Harvard University, 1989.

20. Francis Green, "The Effect of Occupational Pension Schemes on Saving in the United Kingdom: A Test of the Life Cycle Hypothesis," *Economic Journal* 91, 1981, pp. 136–44.

21. Ronald Krumm and Nancy Miller, "Household Savings, Homeownership, and Tenure Duration," Office of Real Estate, Research Paper #38, 1986.

22. For a survey, see Richard H. Thaler, "Anomalies, Saving, Fungibility, and Mental Accounts," *Journal of Economic Perspectives* 4, no. 1, Winter 1990.

23. Martin Feldstein, "Does the United States Save Too Little?" *American Economic Review* 67, no. 1, February 1977, pp. 116–21.

24. See Sanford J. Grossman, Angelo Melino, and Robert J. Shiller, "Estimating the Continuous-Time Consumption-Based Asset-Pricing Model," *Journal of Business and Economic Statistics*, July 1987.

25. Rajnish Mehra and Edward C. Prescott, "The Equity Premium: A Puzzle," *Journal of Monetary Economics* 15, no. 2, March 1985, pp. 145–61.

26. The wealth to income ratio in Japan was, however, still lower than the ratio in the United States as recently as 1987 if we exclude land from wealth. See Fumio Hayashi, "Is Japan's Saving Rate High?" *Federal Reserve Bank of Minneapolis Quarterly Review*, Spring 1989, pp. 3–9. The high value of Japanese land is not the result of accumulated purchases of land by the Japanese.

27. Stephen A. Marglin, "The Social Rate of Discount and the Optimal Rate

of Investment," *Quarterly Journal of Economics* 77, no. 1, February 1963, pp. 97–98.

## CHAPTER SEVEN

1. Michael T. Jacobs, *Short-Term America: The Causes and Cures of our Business Myopia* (Boston, Mass.: Harvard Business School Press, 1991).

2. Shlomo Benartzi and Richard H. Thaler, using the prospect theory of psychologists Daniel Kahneman and Amos Tversky, have shown how a tendency to look at short-term returns profoundly affects the way investors behave. Shlomo Benartzi and Richard H. Thaler, "A Behavioral Explanation of the Risk Premium Puzzle" (reproduced), Cornell University, 1992; Daniel Kahneman and Amos Tversky, "Prospect Theory: An Analysis of Decision Under Risk," *Econometrica* 47, 1979, pp. 263–91.

3. A principal conclusion of the Committee on Time Horizons and Technology Investments of the National Academy of Engineering was that the federal government should encourage longer investment time horizons by tax policy changes to lower the cost of capital. See National Academy of Engineering, Committee on Time Horizons, *Time Horizons and Technology Investments*, Washington, D.C., 1992.

# Bibliography

Ando, Albert, and Alan J. Auerbach. "The Cost of Capital in the United States and Japan: A Comparison." *Journal of Japanese and International Economies* 2 (1988): 134–58.

Auerbach, Alan, and Laurence Kotlikoff. "Demographics, Fiscal Policy, and U.S. Savings in the 1980's." National Bureau of Economic Research Working Paper No. 3150, 1990.

Bain, Andrew. "Short-Termism: The Wrong Diagnosis." *Accountancy* (August 1987): 38–39.

Baumol, William. "Speculation, Profitability and Stability." *Review of Economics and Statistics* 39 (1957): 263.

Bebchuk, Lucian Arye, and Lars Stole. "Do Short-Term Managerial Objectives Lead to Under- or Over-Investment in Long-Term Projects?" National Bureau of Economic Research Technical Working Paper No. 98, March 1991.

Belliveau, Nancy. "Are Pension Administrators Monitoring their Managers to Death?" *Institutional Investor* (January 1974): 81–86.

Benartzi, Shlomo, and Richard H. Thaler. "A Behavioral Explanation of the Risk Premium Puzzle." Cornell University, 1992. Reproduced.

Berle, Jr., Adolf A., and Gardiner C. Means. *The Modern Corporation and Private Property*. New York: The Macmillan Company, 1932.

Bernheim, B. Douglas. *The Vanishing Nest Egg: Reflections on Saving in America*, a Twentieth Century Fund Paper. New York: Priority Press Publications, 1991.

Bhide, Amar. "Active Markets, Deficient Governance." Harvard Business School, 1991. Reproduced.

**126** ◆ WHO'S MINDING THE STORE?

Black, Bernard S. "Shareholder Passivity Reexamined." *Michigan Law Review* 89 (December 1990): 520–608.

Blanchard, Olivier, and Mark Watson. "Bubbles, Rational Expectations, and Financial Markets." In *Crises in the Economic and Financial Structure.* Edited by Paul Wachtel. Lexington, Mass.: Lexington Books, 1981.

Brancato, Carolyn Kay. "Institutional Investors and Corporate America: Conflicts and Resolutions: An Overview of the Role of Institutional Investors in Capital Markets and corporate Governance." In *Impact of Institutional investors on Corporate Governance, Takeovers, and the Capital Markets.* U.S. Congress. Senate. Hearing before the Subcommittee on Securities of the Committee on Banking, Housing and Urban Affairs. Washington, D.C.: U.S. Government Printing Office, 1990.

———, and Patrick A. Gaughan. "The Growth of Institutional Investors in U.S. Capital Markets." Institutional Investor Project, Columbia Center for Law and Economic Studies, 1988. Reproduced.

Brenner, Reuven. *Betting on Ideas: Wars, Inventions, Inflation.* Chicago: The University of Chicago Press, 1985.

Carroll, Chris, and Lawrence H. Summers. "Consumption Growth Parallels Income Growth: Some New Evidence." Department of Economics, Harvard University, 1989. Reproduced.

Case, Karl E. "The Market For Single Family Homes in Boston." *New England Economic Review* (1986): 125–37.

———, and Robert J. Shiller. "The Behavior of Home Buyers in Boom and Post-Boom Markets." *New England Economic Review* (1988): 29–46.

Chan, Su Han, John D. Martin, and John W. Kensinger. "Corporate Research and Development Expenditures and Share Value." *Journal of Financial Economics* 26 (August 1990): 255–76.

Christiano, Lawrence J. "Understanding Japan's Saving Rate: The Reconstruction Hypothesis." *Federal Reserve Bank of Minneapolis Quarterly Review* (Spring 1989): 10–25.

Coffee, John C., Jr. "Liquidity Versus Control: The Institutional Investor as Corporate Monitor." *Columbia Law Review* 91, no. 6 (1991): 1277–1368.

Colm, Gerhard. *Essays in Public Finance and Fiscal Policy.* New York: Oxford University Press, 1955.

Confederation of British Industry. "Short-Termism." (October 1987). Reproduced.

Courant, Paul, Edward Gramlich, and John Laitner. "A Dynamic Micro Estimate of the Life Cycle Model." In *Retirement and Economic Behavior.* Edited by Henry J. Aaron and Gary Burtless. Washington D.C.: The Brookings Institution, 1986.

Deaton, Angus. "Saving in Developing Countries: Theory and Review." *Proceedings of the World Bank Annual Conference on Development Economics 1989.* Washington D.C.: International Bank for Reconstruction and Development, 1990.

DeBondt, Werner, and Richard Thaler. "Does the Stock Market Overreact?" *Journal of Finance* 39 (1985): 793–805.

De Long, J. Bradford, Andrei Shleifer, Lawrence Summers, and Robert J. Waldman. "Noise Trader Risk in Financial Markets." *Journal of Political Economy* 98 (1990): 703–38.

Diba, B., and H. Grossman. "Rational Bubbles in Stock Prices?" National Bureau of Economic Research Working Paper No. 1779, 1985.

Dobson, John. "Sustaining Global Corporate Culture: A Challenge for the 1990s." *Business in the Contemporary World* (Spring 1990): 90–97.

Economic Planning Agency (Keizai Kikakucho). *Financial System in a Time of Reform* (Henkakuki no kin'yu sisutemu). Tokyo: Economic Planning Agency, June 1989.

Eisner, Robert. "Capital Shortage: Myth and Reality." *American Economic Review* 67, no. 1 (February 1977): 110–15.

Ellsworth, Richard R. "Capital Markets and Competitive Decline." *Harvard Business Review* (September/October 1985): 171–83.

———. "Subordinate Financial Policy to Corporate Strategy." *Harvard Business Review* (November/December 1983): 170–82.

Emery, Henry C. *Speculation on the Stock and Produce Exchanges of the United States.* New York: Columbia University Faculty of Political Science, Studies in History, Economics and Public Law, 1896.

Estrella, Arturo. "Consistent Margin Requirements: Are They Feasible?" *Federal Reserve Bank of New York Quarterly Review* 13, no.2 (Summer 1988): 61–79.

Fama, Eugene F. "The Behavior of Stock Market Prices." *Journal of Business* 38 (1965): 34–105.

———. "Efficient Capital Markets: A Review of Empirical Work." *Journal of Finance* 24 (1970): 383–417.

Fama, Eugene F., and Kenneth R. French. "Dividend Yields and Expected Stock Returns." *Journal of Financial Economics* 22 (1988): 3–25.

———. "Permanent and Temporary Components of Stock Prices." *Journal of Political Economy* 96 (1988): 246–73.

Farrell, J. "Profitable Speculation." *Economica* 33 (1968): 183–93.

Feldstein, Martin. "Does the United States Save Too Little?" *American Economic Review* 67, no. 1 (February 1977): 116–21.

Financial Executives Institute. Committee on Investment of Employee Benefit Assets. "Survey of Pension Fund Investment Practices." 1990. Reproduced.

Flynn, John T. *Security Speculation: Its Economic Effects*. New York: Harcourt, Brace & Co., 1934.

Friedman, Milton. *Essays in Positive Economics*. Chicago: University of Chicago Press, 1953.

Fromson, Brett Duval. "The Big Owners Roar." *Fortune* 122 (July 30, 1990): 66–78.

Froot, Kenneth A., James F. Gammil, Jr., and Andre F. Perold. "New Trading Practices and the Short-Run Predictability of the S&P 500." In *Market Volatility and Investor Confidence*. New York Stock Exchange, 1990.

Froot, Kenneth A., Andre F. Perold, and Jeremy C. Stein. "Shareholder Trading Practices and Corporate Investment Horizons." National Bureau of Economic Research Working Paper No. 3638, March 1991.

Froot, Kenneth A., David Scharfstein, and Jeremy Stein. "Herd on the Street: Informational Inefficiencies in a Market with Short-Term Speculation." Harvard Business School, 1990. Unpublished paper.

Gallant, A. Ronald, Peter E. Rossi, and George Tauchen. "Stock Prices and Volume." Working Paper Series on Economics and Econometrics, No. 90–82, Graduate School of Business, University of Chicago, January 1990.

Gately, Dermot. "Individual Discount Rates and the Purchase of Energy Using Durables: Comment." *Bell Journal of Economics* 11 (1980): 373–74.

Gennotte, Gerard, and Hayne Leland. "Market Liquidity, Hedging, and Crashes." *American Economic Review* 80 (December 1990): 999–1021.

Gibson, George R. *The Stock Exchanges of London, Paris, and New York*. New York: G. P. Putnam and Sons, 1889.

Gilson, Ronald J., and Reinier Kraakman. "Reinventing the Outside Director: An Agenda for Institutional Investors." *Stanford Law Review* 43 (1991): 863.

Goetzman, William N., and Roger G. Ibbotson. "Do Winners Repeat? Patterns in Mutual Fund Behavior." Columbia University, 1990. Unpublished paper.

Graham, Benjamin, and David L. Dodd. *Security Analysis*. New York: McGraw-Hill Book Company, 1934.

Graves, Samuel B., and Sandra A. Waddock. "Ownership at a Distance: Implications of Activist Institutional Investors." *Business in the Contemporary World* (Spring 1990): 83–89.

Green, Francis. "The Effect of Occupational Pension Schemes on Saving in the United Kingdom: A Test of the Life Cycle Hypothesis." *Economic Journal* 91 (1981): 136–44.

Grossman, Sanford J. "Insurance Seen and Unseen: The Impact on Markets." *Journal of Portfolio Management* (Summer 1988): 5–8.

———, Angelo Melino, and Robert J. Shiller. "Estimating the Continuous-Time Consumption-Based Asset-Pricing Model." *Journal of Business and Economic Statistics* 5 (July 1987): 315–29.

———, and Merton Miller. "Liquidity and Market Structure." *Journal of Finance* 43 (1988): 617–33.

Hansell, Saul. "Is the World Ready for Synthetic Equity?" *Institutional Investor* (August 1990): 54–61.

Hansen, Lars Peter, and Kenneth J. Singleton. "Stochastic Consumption, Risk Aversion, and the Temporal Behavior of Asset Returns." *Journal of Political Economy* 91 (1983): 249–65.

Hardouvelis, Gikas, and Steve Peristiani. "Do Margin Requirements Matter? Evidence from U.S. and Japanese Stock Markets." *Federal Reserve Bank of New York Quarterly Review* (Winter 1989/90): 16–35.

Hart, Oliver, and David Kreps. "Price Destabilizing speculation." *Journal of Political Economy* 94 (October 1986): 927–52.

Hausman, Jerry. "Individual Discount Rates and the Purchase and Utilization of Energy-Using Durables." *Bell Journal of Economics* 10 (1979): 33–54.

Hayashi, Fumio. "Is Japan's Saving Rate High?" *Federal Reserve Bank of Minneapolis Quarterly Review* (Spring 1989): 3–9.

Hendricks, Darryll, Jayendu Patel, and Richard Zeckhauser. "Hot Hands in Mutual Funds: The Persistence of Performance, 1974–87." John F. Kennedy School of Government, Harvard University, May 1990. Unpublished paper.

Hodder, James E., and Adrian E. Tschoegl. "Some Aspects of Japanese Corporate Finance." *Journal of Financial and Quantitative Analysis* 20, no. 2 (June 1985): 173–91.

Hoey, Richard B., David Rolley, and Helen Hotchkiss. *Decision-Makers' Poll.* New York: Drexel Burnham Lambert, Inc., 1988.

Horiuchi, Akiyoshi, Frank Packer, and Shin'Ichi Fukuda. "What Roles Has the 'Main Bank' Played in Japan." *Journal of Japanese and International Economies* 2 (1988): 159–80.

Hoskins, W. Lee. "Reforming the Banking and Thrift Industries: Assessing Regulation and Risk." Frank M. Engle Lecture, The American College, Bryn Mawr, Pennsylvania, 1989.

Hsieh, David A., and Merton H. Miller. "Margin Requirements and Stock Market Volatility." *Journal of Finance* 45 (March 1990): 3–29.

Jacklin, Charles, Allan W. Kleidon, and Paul Pfleiderer. "Underestimation of Portfolio Insurance and the Crash of October, 1987." Working Paper No. 1098, Graduate School of Business, Stanford University, 1990.

Jacobs, Michael T. *Short-Term America: The Causes and Cures of our Business Myopia.* Boston, Mass.: Harvard Business School Press, 1991.

Janis, I. L. *Victims of Groupthink.* Boston: Houghton Mifflin, 1972.

Jansson, Solveig. "The Fine Art of Window Dressing." *Institutional Investor* (October 1983): 139–40.

Jensen, Michael. "Eclipse of the Public Corporation." *Harvard Business Review* (September/October 1989): 61–74.

Jones, Jonathan D., J. Harold Mulherin, and Sheridan Titman. "Speculative Trading and Stock Market Volatility." U.S. Securities and Exchange Commission, April 1990. Reproduced.

Kahneman, Daniel, and Amos Tversky. "Prospect Theory: An Analysis of Decision Under Risk." *Econometrica* 47 (1979): 263–91.

Kallick, M., D. Suits, T. Dielman, and J. Hybels. *A Survey of America's Gambling Attitudes and Behavior.* Ann Arbor: Survey Research Center Institute for Social Research, University of Michigan, 1975.

Kaplan, Steven. "The Effects of Management Buyouts on Operating Performance and Value." *Journal of Financial Economics* 24 (October 1989): 217–54.

BIBLIOGRAPHY ◆ 131

Keynes, John M. *The General Theory of Employment, Interest, and Money.* New York: Harbinger, 1964. (First published 1936.)

Knight, Frank. *Risk Uncertainty and Profit.* Boston: Houghton Mifflin, 1921.

Kolb, Robert W., and Ricardo J. Rodriguez. "Friday the Thirteenth: 'Part VII'—A Note." *Journal of Finance* 62, no. 5 (December 1987): 1385–87.

Kotlikoff, Laurence J., and Lawrence H. Summers. "The Role of Intergenerational Transfers in Aggregate Capital Formation." *Journal of Political Economy* 89 (1981): 706–32.

Krumm, Ronald, and Nancy Miller. "Household Savings, Homeownership, and Tenure Duration." Office of Real Estate Research Paper No. 38, 1986.

Kupiec, Paul H. "Do Stock Prices Exhibit Excess Volatility, Frequently Deviate from Fundamental Values, and Generally Behave Inefficiently? If So, Can Anything be Done about It?" Board of Governors of the Federal Reserve System, 1992. Reproduced.

Lee, Charles M. C., Mark Ready, and Paul J. Seguin. "Volume, Volatility, and NYSE Trading Halts." University of Michigan, November 1991. Unpublished paper.

LeRoy, Stephen F., and Richard D. Porter. "The Present Value Relation: Tests Based on Variance Bounds." *Econometrica* 49 (1981): 555–74.

Lichtenberg, F., and D. Siegel. "The Effects of Leveraged Buyouts on Productivity and Related Aspects of Firm Behavior." National Bureau of Economic Research Working Paper No. 3022, June 1989.

Loewenstein, George, and Richard H. Thaler. "Anomalies: Intertemporal Choice." *Journal of Economic Perspectives* 3, no. 4 (Fall 1989): 181–93.

Longstreth, Bevis. "Takeovers, Corporate Governance, and Stock Ownership: Some Disquieting Trends." *Journal of Portfolio Management* (Spring 1990): 54–59.

Lowenstein, Louis. *What's Wrong with Wall Street.* Reading, Mass.: Addison Wesley, 1988.

———. Statement before the U.S. Congress. House. Subcommittee on Domestic Monetary Policy, Committee on Banking, Finance, and Urban Affairs. May 17, 1988.

Mankiw, N. Gregory, David Komer, and David N. Weil. "A Contribution to the Empires of Economic Growth." *Quarterly Journal of Economics* 107, no. 2 (May 1992): 407–37.

132 • WHO'S MINDING THE STORE?

Marglin, Stephen A. "The Social Rate of Discount and the Optimal Rate of Investment." *Quarterly Journal of Economics* 77 (February 1963): 95–111.

Marris, Robin, and Adrian Wood. *The Corporate Economy: Growth, Competition and Innovative Potential.* Cambridge, Mass.: Harvard University Press, 1971.

Marsh, Paul. "Short-Termism." Forthcoming in *The New Palgrave Dictionary of Money and Finance.* London: MacMillan, 1992.

McCauley, Robert N., and Steven A. Zimmer. "Explaining International Differences in the Cost of Capital." *Federal Reserve Bank of New York Quarterly Review* (Summer 1989): 7–28.

McConnell, John J., and Chris J. Muscarella. "Corporate Capital Expenditure Decisions and the Market Value of the Firm." *Journal of Financial Economics* 14 (September 1985): 399–422.

McGowan, William C. "The Hustle-Butt Society." *Business and Society Review* (Spring 1987): 52–54.

McGuire, William J. "The Nature of Attitudes and Attitude Change." In *Handbook of Social Psychology.* Edited by Garner Lindzey and Elliot Aronson. Redding, Mass.: Addison Wesley, 1969.

McMillan, Henry. "The Effects of S&P500 Futures Market Circuit Breakers on Liquidity and Price Discovery." U.S. Securities and Exchange Commission, Washington, D.C., June 24, 1990. Reproduced.

Mehra, Rajnish, and Edward C. Prescott. "The Equity Premium: A Puzzle." *Journal of Monetary Economics* 15, no. 2 (March 1985): 145–61.

Miller, Merton H., John D. Hawke, Jr., Burton Malkiel, and Myron Scholes. "Preliminary Report of the Committee of Inquiry Appointed by the Chicago Mercantile Exchange to Examine the Events Surrounding October 19, 1987." December 1987. Reproduced.

Mitchell, Mark L., and Jeffrey M. Netter. "Triggering the 1987 Stock Market Crash: Antitakeover Provisions in the Proposed House Ways and Means Tax Bill?" *Journal of Financial Economics* 24 (1989): 37–68.

Mizuno, Yuko. "Popularity of Equity Financing Threatening 'Keiretsu' System." *Japan Economic Journal* (December 30, 1989, and January 6, 1990).

Musgrave, Richard A. *The Theory of Public Finance.* New York: McGraw-Hill, 1959.

Myers, Stewart. "Signalling and Accounting Information." National Bureau of Economic Research Working Paper No. 3193, December 1989.

———, and Nicolas Majluf. "Corporate Financing and Investment Decisions When Firms Have Information that Investors Do Not Have." *Journal of Financial Economics* 13 (June 1984): 187–221.

National Academy of Engineering, Committee on Time Horizons, *Time Horizons and Technology Investments*, Washington D.C., 1992.

Nelson-Horchler, Joani. "Are U.S. Workers Lazy?" *Industry Week* (June 10, 1985): 45–52.

New York Stock Exchange. *The Capital Needs and Savings Potential of the United States Economy: Projections Through 1985*. New York, 1974.

———. *Market Volatility and Investor Confidence: Report to the Board of Director of the New York Stock Exchange, Inc.* New York, 1990.

O'Barr, William M., and John M. Conley. *Fortune and Folly: The Wealth and Power of Institutional Investing* (Homewood, Illinois: Business One Irwin, 1992).

Oskamp, Stuart. "Overconfidence in Case-Study Judgments." *The Journal of Consulting Psychology* 29 (1965): 261–65. Reprinted in Daniel Kahneman, Paul Slovic, and Amos Tversky. *Judgment Under Uncertainty: Heuristics and Biases.* Cambridge: Cambridge University Press, 1982.

"Performance Fees Make Headway." *Institutional Investor* 23 (June 1989): 129–30.

Pigou, A. C. *Economics of Welfare.* London: Macmillan, 1934. (First published 1920.)

Poterba, James M., and Lawrence H. Summers. "Mean Reversions in Stock Prices: Evidence and Implications." *Journal of Financial Economics* 22 (1988): 26–59.

Presidential Task Force on Market Mechanisms (Brady Commission). *Report.* Washington, D.C.: U.S. Government Printing Office, 1988.

Quinn, Jennifer, George Sofianos, and William E. Tschirhart. "Program Trading and Index Arbitrage." In New York Stock Exchange. *Market Volatility and Investor Confidence: Report to the Board of Director of the New York Stock Exchange, Inc.* New York, 1990.

Reich, Robert B. "Bailout: A Comparative Study in Law and Industrial Structure." *The Yale Journal of Regulation* 2 (1985): 163–224.

Repetti, James R. "The Use of the Tax Law to Stabilize the Stock Market: The Efficacy of Holding Period Requirements." *Virginia Tax Review* 8 (1989): 591–637.

134 • Who's Minding the Store?

Rohrer, Julie. "Games People Play with Performance Figures." *Institutional Investor* (June 1979): 89–96.

———. "The New Activism at Institutions." *Institutional Investor* (October 1983): 177–97.

Sah, Raaj K. "Social Osmosis and Patterns of Crime." *Journal of Political Economy* 99 (1991): 1272–95.

Scharfstein, David S., and Jeremy C. Stein. "Herd Behavior and Investment." *American Economic Review* 80 (1990): 465–79.

Schwert, G. William. "Why Does Stock Market Volatility Change over Time?" *Journal of Finance* 44 (December 1989): 1115–53.

———. "Stock Market Volatility." In New York Stock Exchange. *Market Volatility and Investor Confidence: Report to the Board of Director of the New York Stock Exchange, Inc.* New York, 1990.

Sharpe, William F. *Investments.* 3rd Edition. Englewood Cliffs, New Jersey: Prentice Hall, 1985.

Sheard, Paul. "The Main Bank System and Corporate Monitoring and Control in Japan." *Journal of Economic Behavior and Organization* 11 (1989): 399–422.

Sherif, Muzafer. "An Experimental Approach to the Study of Attitudes." *Sociometry* 1 (1937): 90–98.

Shiller, Robert J. "Do Stock Prices Move Too Much to be Justified by Subsequent Movements in Dividends?" *American Economic Review* 36 (1981): 291–304. Reprinted in Robert J. Shiller. *Market Volatility.* Cambridge, Mass.: MIT Press, 1989.

———. *Market Volatility.* Cambridge, Mass.: MIT Press, 1989.

———. "Market Volatility and Investor Behavior." *American Economic Review Papers and Proceedings.* May 1990.

———, Fumiko Kon-Ya, and Yoshiro Tsutsui. "Expanding the Scope of Expectations Data Collection: The U.S. and Japanese Stock Markets." Cowles Foundation for Research in Economics Discussion Paper No. 1012. March 1992.

———. "Speculative Prices and Popular Models." *Journal of Economic Perspectives* 4, no. 2 (Spring 1990): 55–65.

———. "Stock Prices and Social Dynamics." *Brookings Papers on Economic Activity* 2 (1984): 457–98. Reprinted in Robert J. Shiller. *Market Volatility.* Cambridge, Mass.: MIT Press, 1989.

—, and William J. Feltus. "Fear of a Crash Caused the Crash." *The New York Times*, October 29, 1989.

Shleifer, Andrei, and Robert Vishny. "Equilibrium Short Horizons of Investors and Firms." *American Economic Review* 80 (May 1990): 148–53.

Simon, Herbert. "Behavioral Economics." In *The New Palgrave*. Edited by John Eatwell, Murray Milgate, and Peter Newman. London: Macmillan, 1988.

Simon, William E. *Tax Reform*. Public Hearings on the subject of tax reform before the U.S. Congress. House. Committee on Ways and Means. 94th Cong., 1st sess., pt. 5. Washington, D.C., July 31, 1975.

Smart, Scott B., and Joel Waldfogel. "Measuring the Effect of Restructuring on Corporate Performance: The Case of Management Buyouts." Indiana University, 1991. Reproduced.

Stein, J. "Efficient Capital Markets, Inefficient Firms: A Model of Myopic Corporate Behavior." *Quarterly Journal of Economics* 104 (November 1989): 655–69.

—. "Informational Externalities and Welfare-Reducing Speculation." *Journal of Political Economy* 95 (1987): 1123–25.

Summers, Lawrence H. "Does the Stock Market Rationally Reflect Fundamental Values?" *Journal of Finance* 41 (1986): 591–601.

—, and Victoria P. Summers. "When Financial Markets Work Too Well: A Cautious Case for a Securities Transactions Tax." *Journal of Financial Services Research* 3 (December 1989): 261–86.

Thaler, Richard H. "Anomalies, Saving, Fungibility, and Mental Accounts." *Journal of Economic Perspectives* 4 (Winter 1990): 193–206.

Tirole, J. "Asset Bubbles and Overlapping Generations." *Econometrica* 53 (1985): 1499–1528.

Tobin, James. "The Case for Preserving Regulatory Distinctions." In The Federal Reserve Bank of Kansas City. *Restructuring the Financial System*. 1987.

—. "On the Efficiency of the Financial System." *Lloyds Bank Review* (July 1984): 1–15.

—. "Deposit Insurance Must Go." *Wall Street Journal*, November 22, 1989.

U.S. Bureau of Economic Analysis. *A Study of Fixed Capital Requirements of the U.S. Business Economy 1971–1980*. Washington, D.C., December 1975. (Prepared under the direction of Beatrice N. Vaccara.)

U.S. Congress. Senate. Committee on Banking, Housing, and Urban Affairs. Subcommittee on Securities. *The Impact of Institutional Investors on Corporate Governance, Takeovers, and the Capital Markets.* Washington, D.C.: U.S. Government Printing Office, 1990.

U.S. Securities and Exchange Commission. The Office of Economic Analysis. "Institutional Ownership, Tender Offers, and Long-Term Investments." Washington, D.C., April 19, 1985.

Wallace, Anise. "Hiring High and Firing Low." *Institutional Investor* (September 1979): 53–69.

West, Kenneth. "Bubbles, Fads, and Stock Price Volatility Tests: A Partial Evaluation." *Journal of Finance* 43 (1988): 648–50.

Williamson, Oliver E. *Markets and Hierarchies*. New York: Free Press, 1975.

Yankelovich, Daniel, and John Immerwahr. *Putting the Work Ethic to Work: A Public Agenda Report on Restoring America's Competitive Vitality*. New York: Public Agenda Foundation, 1983.

# Index

Accountability of corporate management, 7

Accounting rules: for encouraging relational investing, 6; for financial disclosure, 24

Ando, Albert, 98

Anti-takeover laws, state, 25, 41, 81

Asset markets, volatility of, 13

Auerbach, Alan, 98, 100

"Autokinetic effect" experiment, 47

Bebchuk, Lucian Arye, 65

Behavioral bubbles, 54–57

Behavioral theories of financial markets, 45, 46–49

Belliveau, Nancy, 72–73

Bentsen, Senator Lloyd, 39

Berle, Adolf A., Jr., 75

Bernheim, B. Douglas, 101

Bhide, Amar, 60

Black, Bernard, 93

Blue Chip Economic Indicators, 34

Boards of directors: decisions about corporate future, 3; pension decision of, 71

Brady Commission, 91

Bubbles: behavioral, 54–57; rational, 53–54

Bull markets, 99

Buyouts, financed with junk bonds, 42

Capital, cost of, and saving rate, 15

Capital Choices, 11

Capital gains tax, 6, 87–89, 107; graduated, 11, 17; on pension funds, 88; recommendations concerning, 21; reform of, 10

Chicago Mercantile Exchange, 91

Christiano, Lawrence J., 101

Circuit breakers, 91–92

Coffee, John C., 93

Collars for trading halts, 16

Commodities Futures Trading Commission, 29

Compulsive gambling, 46

Conglomerates, 78–79; failure of, 74

Conley, John, 68

Control, separation from ownership, 75–79

Corporate democracy, 6, 9; problems with, 18–19; Corporate governance, 8–9; encouraging shareholder participation in, 92–93; real and ideal, 14; recommendations on, 17–20; reforms of, 5

Corporate income tax, deductions for interest, 11

Corporate management: decisions about corporate future, 3; monitoring of, 6; selection and rewards of, 7

Corporate profits tax, 110

Corporate treasurer, 71
Corporation culture, 5, 76
Council on Competitiveness, 11
Crash: of 1929, 89–90; of 1987, 15, 33, 84; of 1987, and margin requirements, 109
Credit conditions, and market price, 50
Cross-corporate stock holdings, 20
Cultural anthropological study of long-term views, 68
Culture, and savings, 102

DeBondt, Werner, 52
Debt: taxes on, 11; tax treatment of, 21, 24; treatment of, corporate, 7
Decision horizons, current, 5
De Long, Bradford, 99
Demographics, and savings, 101
DePodwin, Horace J., 7, 10, 20, 24
Deregulation: of savings and loans institutions, 42; and turnover in stocks, 83–84
Derivative financial markets, 61; and short-term speculation, 82–83
Derivative instruments, 40–41, 90, 107–108
Destabilization of the market by rigid trading strategies, 15–16
Disclosure of executive pay and benefits, 6
Discount rate: and economic well-being, 96; and saving rates, 95–99; and short-termism, 110
Dissent, 23
Dividends, tax treatment of, 10
Dodd, David L., 37
Dynamic inconsistency in discount rates, 98

Economic equilibrium, multiple points of, 53
*Edgar v. MITE Corp.*, 81
Efficient-markets theory, 34–35, 45, 49–53; and investor behavior, 58

Efficient-market theory, 108–109
Equity: taxes on, 11; tax treatment of, 21; treatment of, in corporate taxation, 7
"Equity premium puzzle," 103
Ethical standards, decline in, 42
Excessive Churning and Speculation Act of 1989, 40, 88

Fama, Eugene F., 52
Federal Reserve System, 29; and margin requirements, 109
Feedback, and theories of market behavior, 55
Feldstein, Martin, 102
Feltus, William, 56
Financial Executives Institute Committee, 67–68
Financial instruments, discount rate of, 95
Financial intermediaries, non-bank, 19
Financial management, 13
Financial markets: ideal versus real, 12–14; liquid, 4
Financial research, government subsidy for, 110
Financial speculation, 29–31
Fitts, C. Austin, 11
Flynn, John T., 50
Focal point for a market event, 56–57
"Follow the crowd" thinking, 47
Forecasting returns, 52
Free cash flow, payout of, 80
French, Kenneth R., 52
Friedman, Benjamin M., 10, 11
Froot, Kenneth A., 83
Full disclosure, and corporate democracy, 9
Futures markets, 40, 41, 90

Gambling, 46
Gammil, James F., Jr., 83
Gately, Dermot, 98
Gennotte, Gerard, 34

## INDEX • 139

Germany, example of, 19
Gibson, George, 49
Gilson, Ronald, 93
Government, encouragement of savings, 103–104
Graham, Benjamin, 37
Grant, James, 10
Graves, Samuel B., 78
Grossman, Sanford J., 34–35
Group-decision problems, 74–75
Groupthink, 74

Hardouvelis, Gikas, 90
Hausman, Jerry, 97–98
Hayashi, Fumio, 100
Holding-period restrictions, 87–89; and speculation, 89
Home mortgage market, and savings, 102
Hostile takeovers, 18, 29, 79–81, 109
Housing booms, 89

Income, growth of, and savings rate, 101–102
Incubator funds, 72
Index arbitrage, 82
Inflation, effects on asset values, 17
Information gap, and speculative behavior, 38
Institutional investors: choice of, 70–71; concern with short-term results, 61; focus on, 107; incentives for long-term investment, 40; liquidity of, 93; and management of firms, 76–77; as members of boards of directors, 93; public of, 72; and short-termism, 62–67; speculative behavior of, 39–40; tactics of, 8
Institutional sclerosis, 74–75
Institutional short-termism, 63–65
Insurance companies, 19
Interest, tax treatment of, 10
Internal Revenue Code, 88

International competition, and long-term perspectives, 4
Investment managers, short-term performance pressure on, 67–70
Investment professionals, moral obligations of, 110
Investment vehicles, 98
Investors: decisions about corporate future, 3; long-term perspective, 4; role in corporate governance, 15; survey on behavior of, 57–58

Jacklin, Charles, 34
Jacobs, Michael T., 92, 108
Janis, Irving, 74
Japan: cost of capital in, 98; example of, 19; savings rates, 100–101; turnover rates in, 63
Jefferson, Thomas, 39
Jensen, Michael, 80
Junk-bond crash, forecasting, and profiting from, 51
Junk bonds, 42, 79–80

Kaplan, Steven, 80
Kassebaum, Senator Nancy, 40, 64, 88, 108
Keiretsu, 77
Keynes, John M., 37, 85
Kleidon, Allan W., 34
Knight, Frank, 54
Kogyo, Toyo, 78
Kon-Ya, Fumiko, 57
Kotlikoff, Laurence, 100
Kraakman, Reinier, 93

Lapses of attention, and decision-making, 48–49
Laws: limiting shareholder participation, 77; multi-constituency, 81–82
Leland, Hayne, 34
LeRoy, Stephen, 52
Leveraged buyouts, 18, 24

Lichtenberg, Frank R., 80
Lifetime consumption profiles, 102
Long-horizon returns, forecastable, 52
Long-run planning, public regard for, 95
Long-term corporate decisions, effect of short-term speculation on, 36
Long-term horizon, encouraging, 108–109
Long-term investment, lack of, 31
Lowenstein, Louis, 41, 60, 62, 92

McCauley, Robert, 98
McGowan, William, 42
Machold, Roland M., 10, 11, 16
Major Market Index, 91
Managers, long-term perspective, 4
Mankew, N. Gregory, 99
Margin requirements, 89–90, 107; versus transactions costs, 90
Marglin, Stephen, 104
Market Mechanisms, Presidential Task Force on, 91
Market overreaction to information, 65–67
Market psychology, and market price, 50
Market volatility, and speculation, 33–38
Matsuda, Kohei, 78
Means, Gardiner C., 75
Merchant banking as a model for relational investing, 19
Money managers, evaluation of, 20
Multi-constituency laws, 81–82, 109
Mutual funds, 19; managers of, 72

National saving rate versus private saving rate, 100
New York Stock Exchange, 91

O'Barr, William, 68
Options, 40
Overconfidence, 48–49

Ownership: of public corporations, 5–6; separation from control, 75–79, 109

Panic, circuit breakers to manage, 91
Pension fund managers, 71; public of, 72
Pension funds, 19; managers of fund for, 13; time frame for calculating performance, 67
Peristiani, Steve, 90
Perold, Andre F., 83
Pfleiderer, Paul, 34
Pigou, A. C., 97, 99, 104
Poison pills, 25, 81
Policy options, 105–110
Porter, Michael E., 11
Porter, Richard, 52
Portfolio insurance programs (computer), 40
Portfolio managers, 13
Poterba, James M., 52
Price bubbles, definition of, 45–46
Price changes: and hostile takeovers, 79; reasons for, 35–36; relationship to economic fundamentals, 49
Price of shares of stock as a kind of discounted value, 96
Private saving rate versus national saving rate, 100
Profit opportunity, and efficient-markets theory, 51
Public policy, 14–15; effectiveness in contributing to the economy, 5

Rabinowitz, Martin J., 4, 9, 11
Random walk, speculative boom path, 55
Rational behavior, and the discount rate, 97–98
Rational bubbles, 53–54
Rational economic behavior, and savings rates, 101
Real in come, change in the 1980s, 3

Recommendations, 5–7

Regulations: to deal with speculation, 85; encouraging relational investing, 6; limiting shareholder participation, 77; securities and credit, 25

Regulatory agencies, Securities and Exchange Commission, 29

Regulatory environment: changes to encourage relational investing, 9; restructured, 20

Relational investing, 6, 8; and corporate democracy, 19

Research and development: investment in, 110; and short-termism, 63–65

Resource allocation, and speculation, 58–59

Ridley, Nicholas, 93

Risk: in corporate investments, 103; versus uncertainty, 54

Rohatyn, Felix, 40

Romer, David, 99

Roosevelt, Theodore, 39

Saving and investment, recommendations concerning, 21

Saving rates: and discount rates, 95–99; encouraging increase in, 10

Savings, 96, 99–104; and short-termism, 110

Savings and loan crisis, 42

Securities and credit regulations, 25

Securities and Exchange Commission, 29; research in short-termism, 64–65

Securities Exchange Act of 1934, 77, 89

Securities market, cost of operation of, 60

Shareholder participation, 10; encouraging, 92–93; laws limiting, 77

Shareholders: constraints on communication among, 20; rights of, 6

Shiller, Robert J., 27

Shleifer, Andrei, 99

Short-short rule, 88, 107

Short-termism, 3, 7, 95, 108; antitakeover laws as a remedy for, 41; and behavioral bubbles, 57–58; and corporate governance, 17–18; and the discount rate, 110; institutional, 63–65; rational, 53; and speculation, 37–38; and speculative behavior, 30–31

Siebert, Muriel F., 16

Siegle, Conald, 80

Small Order Execution System (SOES), 16

Smart, Scott B., 80

Smart money: effect of, 57; and market efficiency, 50–51

Socially optimality, and investment professionals, 60

Social security system, and savings, 102

Sophisticated investors, encouraging participation of, 19

Speculation: and deregulation, 83–84; destabilizing, 83; and economic theory, 45–60; effect of transaction taxes on, 86–87; effects of excesses, 35–37; and market volatility, 33–38; measure for dealing with, 85–93; and resource allocation, 58–59

Speculative behavior, 61–84; as an intellectual process, 107; and volatility of the stock market, 99

Speculative booms, 55

Speculative bubble, effect of capital gains tax on, 88–89

Speculative price changes in corporate equity, 29

Speculative short-term trading, effects of, 106

Speculators, social benefits of activities of, 59

Stamp duties, 86

Stock index futures markets, 90; effects of, 82–83

Stock market, volatility of, 83–84

Stock market crash. *See* Crash
Stole, Lars, 65
Summers, Lawrence H., 52, 60, 99
Summers, Victoria, 60
"Survival of the fittest" in the market, 51
Syron, Richard F., 11

Takeovers, 41, 61–62
Taxation, reform of, 21
Tax environment, changes to encourage relational investing, 9–10
Taxes on speculation, 106
Tax incentives for savings and investment, 99
Tax law: influence on private saving decisions, 15; removal of penalties on intermediaries, 20
Tax rates, changes to deal with speculation, 85
Tax reform to encourage productive investment, 6
Tax rules for encouraging relational investing, 6
Thaler, Richard, 52
Tobin, James, 23–25, 41
Trading: needed changes in, 14; recommendations on, 15–21
Transactions costs versus margin requirements, 90

Transactions taxes, 6, 16–17, 23, 85–87, 107
Tsutsui, Yoshiro, 57
Turnover of shares in the stock markets, 62
"12/24 rule," 67

Uncertainty versus risk, 54

Volatility, 84; and dynamic inconsistency, 98; and margin requirements, 90
Volume of trade, correlation with volatility of prices of stocks, 84
Waddock, Sandra A., 78
Waldfogel, Joel, 80
Waldman, Robert J., 99
Wallace, Anise, 70
Wallman, Steven H., 41
"Wall Street Rule," 7–8, 12–13, 20
Washington, George, 39
Weil, David, 99
Williams Act, 109
Window dressing for a portfolio, 72–74
Work ethic, 42

Zimmer, Steven, 98

# About the Author

R obert J. Shiller is the Stanley B. Resor Professor of Economics, Cowles Foundation, Yale University. He received his Ph.D. in economics from the Massachusetts Institute of Technology in 1972. He is Research Associate of the National Bureau of Economic Research, a fellow of the Econometric Society, and a recent recipient of a Guggenheim fellowship. He has written widely on financial markets, macroeconomics, behavioral economics, and statistical methods. His recent book *Market Volatility* (MIT Press, 1989) was a mathematical and behavioral analysis of price fluctuations in speculative markets.